BLACK GIRL DANGEROUS

ON RACE, QUEERNESS, CLASS AND GENDER

MIA MCKENZIE

BGD PRESS, INC.

First published 2014

by BGD Press, Inc.

Oakland, CA

Copyright © 2014 by Mia McKenzie

All rights reserved.

ISBN-10: 0988628635

ISBN-13: 978-0-9886286-3-2

Library of Congress Control Number: 2014940116

For every Black Girl who dares to speak
and every Black Girl who doesn't.

Contents

Preface

A s I write this, *Black Girl Dangerous* is two years and a few months old. When I started the little Tumblr page that would eventually become a multi-faceted forum featuring nearly 100 writers from several countries and millions of readers from every populated continent on earth, I had no idea what I was getting myself into.

I started *BGD* because I was angry. An ex-girlfriend of mine, a white woman, had told me during an argument that she thought black people were scary. *Sexy*, she said. *But scary, too.* She said there was something dangerous "in [our] eyes." In my rage, I started a Tumblr and named it *Black Girl Dangerous*. On it, I ranted about many experiences of anti-black racism and I included the experience I'd had with my ex. When she found out about it, she got angry. Even though there were little more than a few sentences about her, even though I never mentioned her name at all, anywhere, she, rather than choose not to read it, tried to get Tumblr to take the blog down, claiming it was harassment. It wasn't, and Tumblr refused to take it down. Being a *very* privileged person, unused to not getting her way, she decided to go a different route. She filed for a restraining order against me.

The thing is, though, you can't get a restraining order against someone because they called out your racism on their Tumblr. Since we had formerly dated, though, she could get one by accusing me of domestic violence. So, that's what she did. In order to get a restraining order so that I couldn't talk about her racism online, she *invented* an act of domestic violence that never happened. Nope. You didn't read that wrong.

I won't go into the gory details. It's all a matter of public record. It suffices to say that even though I had fifty pages of evidence proving that she made it up, some of that evidence being *her own words* in emails where we talked about how there had never been any violence in our relationship, she still won.

Looking back, I'm shocked at how confident I was going into that courtroom that day, how sure I was that my *evidence* would trump her *word*. It wasn't until I was in front of the judge, lawyer-less, watching my ex's story change from what she had said in her complaint to whatever story served her best in the moment, and when I objected, hearing the judge say that *it didn't matter if her story changed*, that I realized I was in over my head. Way over. She knew, of course. She knew she only had to walk into the courtroom with her petite white self and her tiny voice and she would win—evidence, and even consistency, be damned.

I remember leaving the courthouse in shock and my friend, Vanessa, who was there as a witness (a witness they never bothered to call), shaking her head, saying, "Damn. The U.S. court system: fighting for 'justice,' one white woman at a time."

Girl.

I felt defeated that day. And for many days after. I thought about all the white women I had known throughout my life who had labeled me angry or aggressive just because I refused to be silent or invisible. I figured they'd all won in that courtroom that morning. I spent a few weeks feeling suicidal. I felt like the truth didn't matter, that it couldn't matter, because in the end I was whatever some white woman said I was. The idea of that made me want to die.

But I didn't die.

Instead, I made a choice.

I decided that instead of being silent in the face of what had happened to me, I would be louder. That instead of becoming invisible, I would become manifest. That instead of being defeated, I would triumph, not just over my ex, but over everyone who ever looked at a black woman and saw someone who *could* be silenced, someone whose story didn't matter, whose voice didn't count because...who's gonna believe some black girl, anyway? I decided that, instead of dying, I would live.

And that I *would* be dangerous. Really dangerous. The kind of dangerous that would make a difference in the world.

From that moment, I put my heart and soul into *BGD*. I admit it: it was revenge. But it quickly became so much more than that. It became a place to speak loudly about oppression, without apology and without fear. I wrote almost a hundred pieces in the first year. Bold pieces. Vulnerable pieces. Pieces that pushed and demanded better, not just for me, but also for my people, for our communities. Very quickly, that little Tumblr grew, from word of mouth, Facebook shares and Tweets alone, into the force that it is today. Very quickly it grew from a scream of anguish into a phenomenon.

It's not a pretty origin story. It's a story of how I survived. How I refused to be silenced. How I refused to die.

Those ugly beginnings have a very happy ending. In just two years, *Black Girl Dangerous* has become a platform for nearly 100 queer and trans writers of color (to-date) to find or reclaim their voices, to speak truth to power, and to tell their own stories of struggle and survival and triumph. All to an audience of several million people from all walks of life, all over the world.

The happy ending isn't just *BGD*'s; it's also mine. The trauma that set this thing into motion could have broken me, could have silenced me, could have made me invisible, could have killed me. But I didn't let it.

Today, my voice is stronger and more powerful than ever.

4

Many people have told me that reading *Black Girl Dangerous* changed their lives. Some of them have told me that it saved them. What I want them to know is this: it saved me, too.

Introduction

I'm often asked why *Black Girl Dangerous* is so successful. The answer is two-fold. First, *BGD* fills a need that queer and trans people of color have to be heard and seen, to have their stories matter. Second, we talk about hard, complicated things—the hardest, most complicated things—in a way that's accessible to non-academics. We say it plain. And with as much courage as we can muster.

The essays in this book are my favorites of the pieces I've written for *BGD* in the last two years. They range in topic from race to queerness to class to gender and sometimes all of those at once. They are both personal and political. Some are funny, some are serious, many are both. Along with the original pieces from *Black Girl Dangerous*, I have included some thoughts on responses to the works, questions that came up and, in some cases, instances where my thinking around the subject changed after the writing of the piece.

What I've noticed while pulling this collection together is that these pieces feel different in manuscript form than they do on a website. In real time, there are things that don't need to be explained because everyone is watching something play out in the moment and feeling things collectively. Taken out of those moments and put into a book, some of the writing feels, while no less relevant and necessary, a little out of place. At least to me. For that reason, I ask that you keep in mind the original form of media for these writings and how that form was and is an important part of the way these issues were approached.

Within these pages are two years worth of my brain working. Two years worth of my experiences. Two years worth of my voice. I speak from my own experience and understanding. My analysis isn't perfect. But it is *mine*. There are other analyses, other opinions, other experiences. Though my opinions are shared by countless others, I don't claim to speak for all queer people of color. I speak for myself.

On Rape, Cages and the Steubenville Verdict

Originally published March 2013

Today, the two 16-year-old football players who were accused of raping a 16-year-old girl in Steubenville, Ohio were found guilty. The boys' emotional reactions to the verdict, including crying in court, led several different CNN personalities to lament that their young lives have been ruined. That's right. With no mention of the rape victim and how her life has been affected by being raped (and having the assault photographed and videotaped and tweeted about by the people who watched it all happening and did nothing), CNN went all boo-hoo for the boys who did it.

Now, I'm no fan of CNN and I wouldn't have expected much. But this is beyond the pale, even for them. And it's a continuation of the rape culture that exists in this country and in this world that has been so highlighted by the Steubenville case, a case which "polarized" Steubenville because, while many folks seem to know that rape is bad, many people there, and elsewhere, seem to think that football is more important than 16-year-old girls not getting sexually assaulted. Rape culture has us always blaming women for rape, whether it's because of how we're dressed or how much we drink or whatever. Somehow, underneath it all, it's always kinda the woman's fault. After all, these men and boys have penises and those things are just so hard to control that it can't possibly be their fault. So, women and girls have to take on the responsibility of not getting raped. Because, you know, boys will be boys and stuff.

It's sickening. Really, it is.

What happened to this girl is horrible. Her life has been affected in serious ways by the unbelievably terrible actions of these boys. And CNN should not be talking as if her pain, her experience, and her life do not exist. It is unconscionable for them to do so and they need to be held to account for it. Elevating the experience of these boys above the experience of their victim is not okay.

But, you know what *is* okay? *Also* feeling sorry for these boys.

Not in the way that CNN did it. Not at the expense of the girl who was raped by these boys. But including these boys in our feelings of sadness *is* okay.

I, unlike many people reacting to today's verdict, am not just thrilled to death that two 16-year-old boys are going to jail.

What they did was terrible. There is no excuse. They have to be two seriously fucked-up kids to have done what they did. But what I know for damn sure is that jail does not fix broken people. It only breaks them harder.

The fact is that once these boys enter the prison system, even in juvenile detention, chances are that they will return to it. It will, with little doubt, fuck them up more than they are already fucked-up. They will not likely emerge from prison as two well-adjusted men who respect women and understand that sexual assault against them is not okay. That's not what prison does for people.

As a Black woman, I am especially not thrilled to death to see another Black boy put in a cage. Black boys are disproportionately put in cages and I'm not happy that it's happening again. What this boy did is terrible and I do not in any way excuse it. **It is inexcusable**. Thinking about it makes me feel crazy and hopeless. But adding another Black body to the Prison Industrial Complex just doesn't make me feel any better about it. It only makes me feel worse.

The system of incarceration is an evil system. There is NOTHING good about it. It does not deter criminal behavior or fix it. It is a severely fucked-up, entirely ineffective, ever-growing, for-profit monster. And there is nothing good about two more people being locked-up in it.

Ma'Lik Richmond and Trent Mays need to be held to account for what they did, that's for damn sure. And the girl who was sexually assaulted by them deserves justice. But justice does not and cannot exist in the system of incarceration, in the practice of putting people in cages. The Prison Industrial Complex continues to grow and grow and grow precisely because when very bad things happen we are all too happy to see the people responsible locked away and few of us ever consider the need to find better and more effective ways to deal with violence within communities.

I do feel sorry for these boys. And not only because they will be put in cages that will not make them any better. I also feel sorry that two 16-year-olds are capable of the things these boys have been found guilty of doing. That makes me deeply, deeply sad. That we have created a world in which, at just 16 years old, and even younger, boys can already hate girls this much. That they can already dehumanize and degrade them. That misogyny is so insidious and so effective as to make 16-year-old boys incapable of respecting this girl, of seeing her as a human being with the right to make her own choices, even when drunk, and the right to remain unviolated, even when passed out. I am sorry for these boys that, at 16, some of their humanity is already gone. The cruelty of kids is not new, and I guess it shouldn't shock me, but this specifically gendered cruelty, at such extreme levels and at such a young age, *is* shocking to me. And I do feel very sorry for these boys.

Just not as sorry as I feel for the girl they raped.

One of the boys, Trent Mays, is actually 17. Also, not all men and boys have penises, and not all people with penises are men or boys.

Afterthoughts:

This piece was surprisingly well received. Despite the tendency toward one-dimensional online discussions of controversial topics like this one, *BGD* readers seemed to be able to hold the complexity of these ideas really well. I am always seeking nuance in my thinking and writing around complicated issues (while always aiming to keep the work accessible to non-academics.)

This piece represents my feminism. It's a feminism that isn't rooted in the systems of racist capitalism that the Prison Industrial Complex represents. It's a feminism that understands that "justice" and "equality" cannot exist within the framework of brutal police forces and dehumanizing prison systems that target black and Latino people. Justice for some but not for others isn't really justice at all. I want a justice for victims of rape and sexual assault that doesn't perpetuate racism, classism and the caging and disposal of people who look like me.

You Mad Yet? On the Murder of Trayvon Martin and the Question of Tipping Points

Originally published July 2013

On Saturday, George Zimmerman was acquitted of all charges in the murder of Trayvon Martin. Or, put another way, white supremacy allowed a man to stalk and murder an unarmed black teenager and walk away. If you don't understand how and why this case was about race, which, I believe, requires only the barest minimum of understanding about the world we live in, then this piece is not for you. I'm not the least bit interested in explaining something so incredibly obvious. If you insist on pretending that none of this is about race, please just excuse yourself from this conversation. You don't deserve to sit at the grown-ups' table.

If you're still reading, I'll assume you don't have your head up your ass and that the role of race in this case is clear to you. Great. Now, since we're all on the same page, my only question is:

Are we mad enough yet?

Because here's the thing: the system didn't fail. The system did precisely what it was designed to do. This is the way it has always worked. The way it worked for Emmett Till 60 years ago, for Rekia Boyd 16 months ago, and for the countless unarmed black and brown people killed by white supremacy before, in between, and after them. This country was built on the dehumanization of people of color—the genocide of the Native American, the enslavement and mass murder of the African. This is what we do. So, the question isn't why. The question isn't how, in 2013, this is still possible. The question is, simply, are we mad enough yet? And if so, what are we prepared to do about it?

Because it's not going to stop. In this country, a black woman, man, or child is killed every 28 hours by a cop or vigilante. Prisons are overflowing with black bodies disproportionately locked up. A year ago, Marissa Alexander was sentenced to 20 years in prison for firing warning shots into the air to protect herself from an abusive husband. A few weeks ago, the Supreme Court ruled against a person's right to remain silent unless we have the wherewithal (the education, the presence of mind, the absence of a cop's foot on our throats, etc.) to make it clear that our silence is intended as an exercise of our rights. A key point of the Voting Rights Act, meant to protect black folks from disenfranchisement, was decimated a couple of weeks ago. Something's happening here. The lives of black people have never been valued much in this country, but there used to be at least a trend towards pretending that they were. Now, it seems, even that's gone.

On Sunday, I marched in a protest over the Zimmerman verdict, with maybe a thousand other people in Oakland. Through all the signs and shouting, I kept wondering if this was all. If a few rallies, a few marches, some windows broken by white manarchists, will be as much as we are willing to do in the face of this sustained assault on our humanity. I wondered if, after a couple of days, the protesting will stop and people will just go home and forget. Again. (Or what if we do push back hard enough to get federal charges brought against Zimmerman? Then what? The goal cannot simply be to see George Zimmerman jailed. One more person in the PIC won't bring Trayvon Martin back, and won't likely do anything to prevent the next Trayvon from meeting the next Zimmerman. The problem is so much bigger than one vigilante. So, what is it that we really want? Changes to the Florida laws that allowed Zimmerman to walk free? Changes to all the laws everywhere in this country that put so much power in the hands of already-powerful and equally brutal forces, such as racist police officers?)

I was reminded that a tipping point of the Civil Rights Movement, the act that finally forced the rest of the country to take seriously what was happening to black folks at the hands of Jim Crow, was four little girls in Birmingham being blown apart in the 16th Street Baptist Church before Sunday school by a bomb set by the Ku Klux Klan. It took that level of evil for the Civil Rights Act of 1964 to be passed ten months later. It took that level of unconscionable violence and hatred for people to get outraged, angry and ashamed enough on a national level for something substantial to be done.

It seems, in 2013, that the killings of our children aren't enough. So, what it's going to take this time?

Dangerous

Originally published January 2012

I'm dangerous.

When I was in second grade, I was given a reading test. The test-giver wasn't my regular teacher, but someone whose job it was to give reading tests, I guess. I was six years old, a year younger than everyone else in my class, because, after having my IQ tested at the age of five, it was recommended that I skip kindergarten and go straight to first grade. I was smart. I was gifted, to be more precise. And I knew it. So, this one day in second grade, I was given a reading test. I sort of remember what the classroom was like, I kind of remember the table where I sat. The test-giver pointed out words to me on a sheet of paper, and I told her what the words were. I don't remember the words now. Except one of them. I remember the word: R.E.A.D.

I knew this word. I knew what this word meant. I knew that the present and past tense of this word were spelled the same and had different pronunciations. (I also knew the word 'pronunciation'.) I had a thing about this word. The thing was that

17

whenever I was presented with this word out of context, outside of a sentence where it had to be either the past or present tense depending on the meaning of the sentence, whenever it was up to me to just decide which tense I wanted the word to be, I always chose the past tense. Simply because I liked the sound of that word better. I liked the sound of [red] better than the sound of [reed]. I still do. It sounds denser, deeper, more soulful, doesn't it? So, when the test-giver pointed at this word, not in a sentence but completely without any context, I knew it could be either the past or present tense and that it was for me to say it whichever way I liked. I said: [red]

I meant: the past tense of read [reed].

The test-giver frowned, and I remember the frown exactly. I had gotten every word right up until then, and the frown was a frown of disappointment, like, "Aw, shucks, you got one wrong."

The test-giver said something like, "No. That word is 'read' [reed]. Not red."

I was six. And I remember thinking: I am smarter than this teacher.

I think that was the moment I became dangerous.

Little black girls are not supposed to be brilliant. So many of us are, but we're not supposed to be. To be a black girl in the world is to be nothing. To be a black girl in the world is to be dismissed and dehumanized at every corner of the globe, every single day. To be brilliant and a black girl is, in many people's minds, an oxymoron. An impossibility.

But I didn't know that then.

In my world, in the world of my family, being a brilliant black girl was not only possible, but an everyday reality. In my family, I was surrounded by smart black women. And I was told all the time that I was smart. I would go so far as to say that as a child my gifts (my intellect as well as my talents) were revered by my family. Every aced test, every starred art project, every perfect memorization of a poem or a bible verse was—to my aunts, my grandmother, my grandfather, my great-grandmother—a holy thing that demanded praise and exaltation.

This is not to say that I was spoiled. I wasn't. My parents were not nearly as impressed with me as my other family members. Or, it might be more accurate to say, they were not as good at showing me that they were impressed. They were very young. They did not always take the time to make me feel special. But I was lucky that I had other family members who did.

My late preadolescence and my early adolescence were awkward. To say the least. I was skinny, and most of my face was nose (it still is). I was teased a lot at school. I was called ugly, a lot. My self-esteem wavered a little in the years between ten and fourteen. But even as I experienced teasing, and sometimes cruelty, about my looks at the hands of other kids, I never forgot that I was smart. Gifted. That idea had been rooted so deeply in me that nothing has ever been able to shake it loose.

It has been the most important idea of my life, the most essential thing I know and have ever known about myself.

The world has tried to make me forget it. Every time I turn on the TV, or the radio, I am reminded that black women are supposed to be crack-addicted welfare-queens, ghetto skanks, and ignorant, ratchet, violent loud-mouths—these are the stereotypes of people who look like me. Every time I interact with a white person who is surprised at how "well" I speak, or a black person who is surprised by how "white" I sound, I am reminded that black women are supposed to fit into the tiny box of white supremacy's expectations of us. Every day, in some way or another, someone assumes I am less than what I am.

But I'm lucky. Because I know what I am.

And knowing makes me dangerous.

Knowing means that I can't be controlled. It means that I can't be shamed or silenced. That I can't be made smaller. It means that no matter what happens, no matter what fucked-up shit anyone says or does (including me), I still love myself. Even when I fail or falter (which I do all the time), even when I am not as good as I hope to be (which I often am not), I still believe in myself.

And to be able to say that while walking around in this world, in this skin, is, I think, an amazing thing.

I am dangerous.

I want to be. If it means that I'm not taking anybody's shit. If it means that I make my voice heard. If it means I'm tough enough to survive, and not only to survive, but to grow, to blossom, to be beautiful and rare. If it means I'm willing to take chances, that I'm willing to RISK, every single day of my life.

I am empowered, now, by the idea of my own dangerousness.

I am inspired by it. I am made new by it, every day.

Afterthoughts:

I almost always share this piece when I travel to colleges and universities. This was one of the first posts ever published on *BGD*, back when it was a Tumblr site. This post says a lot about me, about how I became who I am. Some of the family members I mention in this piece are no longer living, but I thank them every day for the ways they loved me when they were here. It is because of them that I have had the confidence to do all of the amazing things I've been able to do in my life, including *Black Girl Dangerous*.

Love, QPOC Style

Originally published May 2012

Love is challenging in all its forms. Familial love, love in friendship, love in romance. Love in our relationships with ourselves. There are all sorts of definitions for love, all sorts of ideas about what love is. In *All About Love*, bell hooks talks about love "as the will to extend one's self for the purpose of nurturing one's own or another's spiritual growth." I like that definition, it sounds right. And simple enough in the way a definition of love ought to be simple.

Only it isn't simple at all. Because in order to extend one's self for anyone's spiritual growth, including one's own, one has to first be *capable* of extending one's self, and then be *willing to choose* to do so. And extending one's self, for the purpose of anything, let alone love, is really fucking scary.

It's scary for everyone. For us, for queer people of color, it is exceptionally scary. As POC, we are taught by the people in power in this country that we are less, and are therefore less deserving of things like freedom and justice, education and employment, respect of our minds and consideration of our

22

bodies, and, surely, the best thing of all—love. As queers, the messages we get aren't much better. As queers of color...well...

As queers of color, we are both invisible and reviled. This country sees race and sexuality as mutually exclusive. You are black *or* you are gay. You are brown *or* you are a lesbian. White people are the only people allowed to be complex enough to be queer. Because white is the default, the normal, the expected, white people can be anything, and more than one thing simultaneously. The rest of us, not so much. Still, our invisibility doesn't stop us from also being hated. Somehow, we are seen just enough to be abhorred, to be targets. It's a strange space to exist in.

Many of us grow up thinking (because we are told so) that we are not the kind of people who get to be happy. The images of happy people on TV and in movies and magazines look nothing like us. Happiness and its components, of which love is surely a big one, maybe the biggest, are not for us. So, for us to even begin to be able to love, to love the way bell hooks defines it, we have to believe, somehow, in spite of everything that says otherwise, that we are worthy of love, that we deserve to love and be loved. Which is totally possible. But it takes a lot of time, and a lot of hard work. And that work can't even begin until we recognize that we need it, which many of us never do. For those of us who do recognize it, and invest in the hard work of self-healing and growth, it's still really, really challenging.

We come to the table of love with all this baggage, with all these voices in the back of our minds telling us not to bother, not to even try, because we'll never be good enough, and trying will only get us hurt, maybe beyond repair this time. We come anyway. Because we are human and we have to. We want love, even though it terrifies us. So, we come to the table. We come to it together. We ask each other out on dates. We lean in for kisses. We fuck. We feel. And all the time we are waiting for it to not work. All the time we are waiting for the proof that we were right all along, that we don't deserve it. Or we can't wait, the waiting is too much, so we leave first so as not to be the one who is left.

Letting down your guard can be really difficult, especially when you are black or brown and have been taught that letting down your guard is a sure way to not survive in a world that wants to kill you. Still, somehow we find ways to do it, to let each other in, to allow friends and lovers into the deepest parts of our hearts. We get hurt, terribly hurt, by each other. And still, we keep trying.

Sometimes it does work. Sometimes, a lot of the time, we build lasting friendships that see us through the most difficult moments of our lives, and that fill our days with good, good stuff. Sometimes we create lasting monogamous and polyamorous romances. Sometimes, we learn how to really love ourselves, how to extend ourselves for the purpose of our own spiritual growth. We do all of this while carrying the nearly incalculable weight of oppression, while resisting racism and heterosexism and transphobia and xenophobia and colonialism. In the face of all of these things, any one of which by itself should be enough to shut us down, we find ways to love each other more and better. Which really, when you think about it, makes us great at love.

It makes us **superstars of love**.

Because our love for each other *is* love for ourselves. By loving other black and brown queers, in all the ways I love them, I am also loving my Self, healing my Self, rejecting all the bullshit that tells me I'm not worthy, that love is not for me. Every time I trust my friends enough to fail in front of them, every time I commit to some activity of self-care, every time I take a lover's hand when the voices are telling me to just give up because I cannot really have this thing, I am loving all of us.

My life, without my ever deciding it, has become a serious journey of love. QPOC style.

8 Ways Not To Be An Ally

Originally published June 2013

People like to throw around the term "ally". White people who claim to be anti-racist, non-disabled folks who claim to be invested in challenging ableist norms, cis queers who claim to understand the importance of trans* visibility. People claim "ally" for themselves regularly and with ease. But the truth is that being an ally takes more work than most of us imagine. In fact, it takes constant vigilance. And there are many ways we fail at it everyday. Frankly, some of us are just totally doing it wrong.

To help sort it out, I've compiled this list of "8 Ways Not To Be An Ally" and I hope it's useful.

1. Assume one act of solidarity makes you an ally forever.

Remember that time your uncle said that fucked-up stuff about "illegal" Mexican immigrants and you were all, "Actually, Uncle, California *is* Mexico, so you need to read your history cuz that's hella racist!" That shit rocked, bruh. And it totally means

26

that you are an Ally with a capital A for, like, ever! Done and done. Let's go get a celebratory slurpee. But you know what else? Nope. Being an ally takes waaaay more practice than that. It is a constantly active and evolving thing. I mean, imagine labeling yourself a great lover after you ate pussy once. That would be cray, wouldn't it?

2. Make everything about your feelings.

The hurt feelings that resulted when you were called out on racism/transphobia/ableism/etc. are totally more important than the impact of the actions you are being called out for in the first place. Really. I'm not even being facetious. Psych! I mean, I know it *feels* like your feelings are Consideration #1, but they're not. I have been guilty of this ridiculousness myself in the past. I think everybody is guilty of it sometimes. But that still doesn't make it okay. Try to remember that people who have been impacted by your racist/transphobic/ableist/etc. words or actions are the ones whose feelings need attention right then. Not yours.

3. Date 'em all.

Some folks seem to think that the quickest way to lifelong allyship status is to just date all the people who resemble those that one claims to exist in solidarity with. Anti-racist? Date all the

POC! And be sure to do so exclusively and with no analysis whatsoever about fetishism, exotification, or the ways your white body might be interrupting POC space! Cuz, hey, you're an ally and stuff. Right? Ew.

4. Don't see race/gender/disability/etc.

You know what I love? When people don't see my race. There is nothing more affirming for me as a person than to have essential parts of myself and my experience completely disregarded. I mean, inside we're all the same. And there's only one race: the HUMAN race! Amirite??? Ugh. Listen. If your ability to respect someone's right to exist requires pretending that they are just like you, that's a problem. We are not all the same. And things like race, gender, disability, etc. are exactly the kinds of things that shape our lives and our experiences and make us different from one another. Being different is not the problem. The idea that being the same as you is what gives us the right to exist is the problem.

5. Don't try any harder.

You tried, right? You reached out to three different QPOC burlesque performers and asked if they wanted to be in your burlesque show and they all declined. Now your show is as white as a Klan meeting, but it's not your fault, right? You did your part. But now people are mad at you and it makes no sense because *Jesus*! I mean, you totally freaking tried! Here's the thing, though: try harder! If changing the status quo were easy, we'd have done it ages ago.

6. Challenge oppression in personal situations but not in systemic ways.

It's enough that you said something when your Grandma used the T-word. The fact that you go to work everyday at a queer organization where none of the fifty employees are trans* women and you never say nothing about it is beside the point. You're battling interpersonal "isms" and that's what really matters. Except…you know…not really. Transphobia, ableism, racism, and all those other phobias/isms aren't just interpersonal issues. They are hella systemic. And checking your grandma isn't going to fix them. Think bigger, k?

7. Take. Don't give.

To be a great ally, show up at every POC event, read every article about the PIC and comment extensively, and ask endless three-part questions during the Q&A at that symposium on disability justice. And definitely show up extra early for that free QWOC film festival with limited seating so that you for sure get a spot. But never, ever volunteer or donate to help make those things happen.

8. Quote Audre Lorde.

The best way to show solidarity with a group of people is to constantly quote famous folks from that group in regular conversation. Or in Facebook status messages. In fact, you should generally behave as though you know more about the experiences of a group of marginalized people than those people do themselves. That shit is hot. And it totally does not make me want to punch you in the face.

Bacon-Wrapped Donuts and Racism: My Exclusive Interview With Paula Deen

Originally published June 2013

Black Girl Dangerous was invited to sit down with Paula Deen, the celebrity chef who is right now embroiled in a scandal after a former employee accused her of, among other things, racism in the workplace. Deen admitted in a deposition that she has used the N-word and that she is not offended by jokes that use it, stating, "I can't, myself, determine what offends another person."

I met with Deen at her home in Savannah, GA. She invited me to sit at her kitchen table where I was served coffee, and donuts wrapped in bacon, which, I won't even lie, were delicious. Ms. Deen was wearing a simple pink frock and her eyes were as pink as the dress. She'd clearly been crying.

PD: This has all been so upsetting for me. People are saying such terrible, awful things. I don't understand why folks don't think before they speak. Especially in public. You know, you can really hurt someone with your words if you're not careful.

BGD: Are you guilty of the racist behavior you're being accused of?

PD: Oh no! Of course not!

BGD: So, you didn't use the N-word and laugh at jokes at the expense of black people?

PD: Oh, well, yes, I did do those things. Which I am very, very sorry for. But I'm not a racist. I mean, I'm not running around in a white hood burning crosses on some darkie's lawn like some crazy redneck! In fact, there hasn't been a grand dragon of the ku klux klan in my family for generations.

BGD: Generations? Really?

PD: Well, *a* generation, at least.

BGD: A *whole* generation?

PD: Well…a couple weeks for sure. You know what? Let's go ahead and call it eleven days just to be safe.

BGD: But you do understand that racism isn't just a matter of running around in a white hood and burning crosses? That for a white person to use the N-word, and especially to use it in the workplace, *is* racist?

PD: I'm not following you, sweetie. You want some more butter in your coffee?

BGD: Um, no. One pat is enough, thanks. Um, Ms. Deen...actually, can I call you Paula? Ms. Deen carries with it an amount of respect that I feel unable to fake with you right now.

PD: Sure. May I just call you black girl? That's what you go by, right? Also, I've never been any good at remembering nigg—erm, black people's names. They're so strange! Laqueefah and Janeesika and so forth.

BGD: My name is just Mia, though.

PD: *Jusmia*?! Lord! See what I mean?

BGD: On second thought, I think I will have more butter.

PD: You know what's really burning my behind is all these white folks acting like they don't use the word. Most of 'em do. And even if they don't use it, they *think* it. I'll give you an example: you're on the freeway and somebody cuts you off. You look over and see it's a black man. Now, you might not say, *effin' you-know-what*. But most whites, north or south, are gonna *think* it. You see what I'm saying?

BGD: Yes. And I agree with you. Does that excuse you saying it?

PD: Well, yeah, I was kinda hoping it would.

BGD: (rolls eyes)

PD: Listen. What I really want people to understand is that I am a good person. I don't care if you're black, green with purple spots, *super* black with a big ol' nappy afro, Mexican with one of those stinky burrito trucks, or just a normal white person. I will hire anyone to work in my kitchen, as long as they are qualified and don't actually talk to the customers unless they are lighter-skinned than this here brown paper bag.

BGD: Why do you have that in your pocket? You just carry that with you all the time?

PD: Oh, you never know when you're gonna have to do a shade-check. Some black people look deceptively light-skinned when they're standing with a group of darker black people, but then when they are around white people they suddenly look all *blackety*-black. They go from Denise straight to Rudy on the Huxtable scale, you know what I mean? Not that I won't hire a "Rudy"! I'm not saying that. Somebody's gotta wash the dishes, after all.

BGD: Yes, you've also been accused of putting darker-skinned people back in the kitchen and only wanting whites and light-skinned blacks to interact with customers.

PD: Oh, we've been doing that for centuries. My great-great-great grandaddy usedto put all the darker ones out in the fields and all the lighter ones in the house. Everybody did that. That's just tradition.

BGD: Oh God. You're talking about slavery, aren't you?

PD: Oh, I don't like that term. It's so ugly. Such an ugly term for such a beautiful time. Now, I'm not necessarily saying that enslaving a whole race is the right thing to do. But you have to admit, your people never looked classier than they did as house slaves, in their crisp white shirts and bow ties. Am I right?

BGD: (blank stare)

PD: (wide smile)

BGD: How can anyone think that using racial slurs in the workplace is acceptable?

PD: Sugar, I'm from the South. That's just how we talk.

BGD: I know people from the South who definitely don't talk like that.

PD: I mean respectable whites, honey, not ni**er-lovers. Look, I didn't mean anything by it. Everybody knew it was all just joking around. I believe in having a work environment that is lively and fun, where everyone, no matter what color they are, is free to make fun of black people. And really, I love black people, honey. Some of my best coathangers are black. Their names are Rolly and Mr. Jangles. I pay them to stand by the front door of my houses during parties, with their arms out to their sides, and let visitors hang their coats on them. They are delightful people, really. Also, Oprah. I love Oprah! She is such a good ni — erm, she is one seriously upstanding black citizen. Look at how successful she has been, even with that ridiculous black name and big black field-negress behind.

BGD: Oprah has class-privilege. I mean, she's one of the wealthiest people on the planet. What about black folks who aren't rich? Who don't have TV networks? You know, like, the ones who work for you. Do you respect them?

PD: Did you hear what I said about Rolly and Mr. Jangles?

BGD: Yeah, I don't feel like it qualifies.

PD: Well, I don't know what y'all want from me, sugar. I mean, I'm not perfect, but I try, you know? I thought we were supposed to be in a post-racial society anyhow! We did elect Hussein Obama, afterall!

BGD: You voted for Obama?

PD: Oh, hell no. Fuck I look like?

Afterthoughts:

This may be my favorite piece that I've written for *BGD*. I like writing comedy, and particularly satire, a lot. This piece is ridiculous and I absolutely love it. As I write this afterthought, the country's been embroiled in a debate about satire, after Stephen Colbert, on his show *The Colbert Report*, used racist slurs against Asians in yet another skit. The joke was meant to highlight Native American people's demands that the Washington Redskins football team change its offensive name. What it did instead was cause backlash from Asian Americans and others standing in solidarity with them against Colbert, who question whether calling racist jokes 'satire' makes them okay, particularly when they are coming from a white man's mouth. The uproar caused me to call into question the usefulness and validity of white racial satire altogether in a piece entitled, "*On Colbert and White Racial Satire: We Don't Need It.*"

White Silence

Originally published March 2012

I've noticed a trend. When I post to my Facebook page about gay cats, or my friend Sacha (a boy) trying out for the Denver Broncos cheerleaders, or bacon, my Facebook friends respond with comments and likes all across the board. That is to say, the friends who respond are all across the board—black, brown, white, queer, straight, all genders. There is no specific category of friends that responds more or less than any other, when it comes to pretty much anything I post on Facebook.

Except, as it turns out, when I post anything about race.

When I post anything about race, there's a shift in who responds. Suddenly, my white friends are silent. Almost all of them. Every time.

And it's starting to piss me off.

Most of the stuff I post about race is in the form of articles about things going on in the country and in the world, having to do with racism. Most recently, I've been posting links to news and articles about Travyon Martin, the 17 year-old boy who was murdered last month in Florida while walking home with a bag of skittles. He was shot by a self-appointed neigh-borhood watch captain who thought he looked "suspicious" and followed him, accosted him, and shot him in the chest. Anyone who knows about this story, I would think, would be outraged. Scratch that. I know enough to know that there are many people who would not be outraged, many, many people who would not and do not give a shit. But I am not Facebook friends with those people. Or, at least, I didn't think I was.

I am careful about who I friend on Facebook. I keep my friends around 150 or so, because I don't think it's possible to really know more people than that, and I like my bubble, I like to be surrounded by people who share most of my politics. I'm okay with that. I'm almost 36, and I have learned that I don't really need to "appreciate everyone's point of view." I mean, you can have politics that are opposed to mine. Fine. But if you do, we are not going to be *friends*. I think that's reasonable. So, I think my Facebook friends pretty much fall into the category of "people who share my politics," with very few exceptions. They are also people who care about things, people who post about different causes. This includes the white folks on my friends list. My white Facebook friends are mostly liberal democrat/independent types, queer or ally, feminist people who post about those things. And yet, whenever I post about race, they are silent.

Why?

They are people I like, so I want to give them the benefit of the doubt. Maybe they are silent because they don't know what to say. Maybe they feel uncomfortable about chiming in on a subject that is so touchy. Maybe. But a simple "like" doesn't require any comment. A simple "like" would show that you at least read the article, that you at least gave enough of a fuck to follow the link and get informed.

Or maybe they think they don't have a right to comment because they are white and it's not their place. That it's for black people to discuss issues of racism, that they'd be overstepping by commenting. This answer only makes sense if they don't see racism as their problem. If they don't see the oppression of racialized people as part of the history and present of their own country. If they don't know that their involvement in these discussions is necessary, even if it's scary, even if it's hard. Which maybe they don't.

And I guess I shouldn't be surprised, but I am. Again, these are not random white folks. These are my "friends." These are people I like, and who like me. Some of them I even love. I imagine that some of them love me. And yet, when yet another black person is murdered in cold blood, for the crime of being black, or locked up for "stealing" an education for their kid, they don't seem to see that it could have been my brother or my mother. They don't seem to know that it could have been me.

41

Because it *is* me. I have had the experience of being racially profiled a thousand times. I have had a white person characterize me as "violent" for no other reason than a *look* I gave them, for something they "saw in my eyes." I live in a world where I am believed to be dangerous because a white person says I am. Case closed. I have never committed a crime, but I am terrified of the police. Because I know that if one day they decide I did something, whether I did it or not, my life could be over. Just like that. And this is not just true of me. It is true of every black person you know, regardless of gender or age or education level or artistic talents or any other factor. And yet my white "friends" don't seem to know that. They don't seem to understand. They don't seem to want to.

White privilege is a hell of a thing. It makes it possible for my white "friends" to look the other way when a tragedy of as much magnitude as the Trayvon Martin killing happens. If it's too much, they can just choose not to read it, not to think about it. But we don't all have that option.

So, I want to say this to my white friends: I need you to care about this. And I need you to show that you do, by commenting, by sharing, by making noise about this. I need you to be OUTRAGED. Because otherwise, I can't trust you. Otherwise, you are part of the problem. Otherwise, we are not really friends at all.

Afterthoughts:

This was one of the first posts on *BGD* to go viral. It was widely read and shared. Looking back at this piece now is pretty strange for me because my thoughts and feelings about white "allyship" have changed dramatically in the last two years. Ironically, this post is probably where the change started.

Some white readers read this post and filtered it through the lens of white privilege. They decided I was telling them that their thoughts and feelings about racism were just as important as those of POC, just as valid, so they could and should take up the same kind of space as POC when talking about these issues. Which, of course, is not what I wrote.

Some white readers' misreading of much of this piece prompted a follow-up (*White Silence: A Follow Up*) in which I explain in further detail exactly what "allyship" on Facebook ought to look like. I was pretty annoyed at having to do that. It was maybe the first time I felt deeply that "educating" white people wasn't a good way for me to spend my energy. Over the next two years, that feeling would grow into a solid stance on so-called "allyship" and its importance, and the wisdom of prioritizing the "education" of privileged people.

White Silence: A Follow-Up

Originally published March 2012

There have been many, many views of my post on white silence, many re-blogs, and much discussion, and I just want to clarify a few things:

I am not calling for "commentary" from my white friends about issues of race. I am not calling for my white friends to tell me that they understand what it is like for folks of color in this country and in this world. I am not calling for my white friends to suddenly start acting like experts on these issues, or, God forbid, to stop listening in order to start talking.

What I am asking is that my white friends show me that they care about these issues by reading, re-posting articles (written by people who DO understand), writing supportive comments (not commentary), and showing their OUTRAGE.

Some examples:

"This is terrible. I am re-posting!"

"Racism sucks!"

"I read this and it made me so angry and sad. Post-racial society my ass!"

And so on.

No one, least of all me, is calling for white people to tell people of color what's what about experiences they can't understand. That is a BAD idea. Shutting up when you don't know what you're talking about is a GOOD idea.

So, here are two very, very important things you can do:

1. Help to create space where people of color can make their voices heard. You can do this by posting and reposting articles written by POC, and written about racism and social injustices. You can also do this by making supportive comments about those posts.

2. Educate yourself on the realities of racism, so that you can understand your own privilege. Then you can talk to OTHER WHITE PEOPLE about their privilege, and check them when they are being racist.

This will help a lot. Really, I promise you.

Also, if your response to the original post sounds anything like, "I'm white and whenever I talk about racism, people get mad at me, and it really hurts my feelings, so I just stay out of it, wah wah wah," please check your privilege. Racism is a tough subject for ALL OF US. The fact that you get to "opt out" to protect your feelings shows how white you are. The rest of us don't have that option. When we talk about racism, we are told to shut up. We are told that we are over-reacting, or that we are seeing things that aren't there. We are told to get over it, because slavery ended years ago and we have a black President. We are insulted and demeaned. And we keep talking anyway. Because we don't have a choice. If you understand that racism is your problem, too, then you understand that you shouldn't have a choice, either.

Racism is your problem. Act like you know that.

On 'Accidental Racism' and Forgetting

Originally published April 2013

There's a lot to say about the Brad Paisley and LL Cool J song "Accidental Racist" and everything it brings up. Like the fact that being an "accidental" racist is not a thing. Doing racist stuff, whether 'accidentally' or on purpose, is just plain old 'being racist'. So there's that. Plus a whole bunch of other things. Way too much, really, to attempt to tackle in a single post. Maybe I'll write more about it in the future, but right now I just want to say a few words (relatively speaking) about a couple of things.

I've been thinking about this "Accidental Racist" thing for a few days now. If you don't know, it's a song by Brad Paisley and LL Cool J about race relations and how, basically, we should all just get over slavery and Jim Crow and, you know, the entire history of racism in this country and not be mad at Brad Paisley for wearing confederate flags on his clothing. My first reaction to it was "Bwahahaaaahaaaa!!! What were these

47

dumbasses thinking and how did they get to be so damn stupid?" I mean, it's hard to get too worked up about a bad country song that's partly a bad rap song with an almost unbelievably bad take on a subject as serious as racism. It just seemed like a ridiculous joke. I was all, "LL, you peaked at 'Round The Way Girl', homie."

But then I remembered how often I hear many of the sentiments that are expressed in this ridiculous song, particularly as editor of *Black Girl Dangerous*. While most of our regular readers are people who have at least some analysis on race, often random folks of all races stop in to say incredibly stupid shit on the subject. A few weeks ago, a dude actually commented that he had "lost [his] white privilege long ago" because he was a long-haired hippie and had spent time in prison. Yeah, he was still white, though. And in response to "How to Be a Reverse Racist," a satire meant to highlight the reasons why racism against white people can't exist (because it's a system of oppression and stuff), a Black person accused me of being racist against white people. Yep, that happened. Thinking about it, and adding the Paisley/Cool J song on top of it, I realized (what I already knew, of course) that those of us who understand what racism is, understand the insidious ways it operates, and understand its effects in all their complexity are in the very, very small minority. And the people who don't really understand any of it...well, they outnumber us by the *millions*.

That thought depressed me. And for a day or so I thought this Paisley/Cool J collab was maybe signaling the end of the world. Because if we're in 2013 and people are writing songs like this, it makes you wonder if anything legitimate we've ever said about racism has even been heard. And if it hasn't, I feel it's safe to say that humanity as a whole is just a bunch of intellectual cavepeople with no real capacity for learning or growth and is just a total lost cause at this point. And I was like, 'fuck it' and watched 4 hours of *Smash*.

Then something happened that brought it all back again. My friend who works at a cafe told me about an incident where a young Black boy of about 15 years walked into the cafe and was immediately approached and harassed by the owner, a white man who is always doing stuff like that. The kid was doing nothing but existing, breathing, blinking, etc. and the owner was so sure that he was some kind of threat that he got all up in his space and asked him what he was doing there and basically harassed him until he was shaken and angry and sad. The owner, who, again, has done this stuff before, thinks he's protecting his staff and his customers from anyone who looks "suspicious". And surely if called out he would say it wasn't about race. And if anyone pointed out that he only does it to Black males, and that's racist, he might say it was "accidental".

In other words, racism isn't his intention, he's just busy protecting his cafe and racism is some kind of by-product. But guess what? NO.

There is nothing "accidental" about making a bee-line for a Black boy because he looks suspicious to you. That is some George Zimmerman shit. That is some very usual, very run-of-the-mill, is-happening-all the-time somewhere, straight-up racist shit. And you know what else it is? It is a CHOICE. While you may not have complete control over what you *feel* when you are confronted by something that makes you uncomfortable (for whatever ingrained racist reason it does), you certainly have a choice about what actions you take. And harassing a kid because he's Black and his pants are sagged is a bad choice. A racist choice. Just like wearing a confederate flag on your t-shirt is a choice, Brad Paisley. If you know what the flag is and what it represents and you still put it on your body and walk around in it and get in front of a camera wearing it, that's not an accident. You didn't trip over the corner of the rug and fall into the shirt. You made a choice. A really, really racist one.

This whole idea that racism is something that happened in the past and that we should all 'get over it' is so absurd on so many levels, not the least of which is that IT'S NOT IN THE PAST. Racism—in particular anti-Black and anti-Brown racism—is a system of oppression and violence that continues, every single day in every single place across this country. It happened in that cafe yesterday and it's happening right now in cafes and on streets and in corporations and on movie sets. Black people are killed and caged every day for *being Black*. Honestly, that kid in the cafe got off easy. At least no one put him in handcuffs or shot him.

"Accidental Racist" is more than just a joke of a song. It's an example of the ignorance of Americans and the unwillingness to even try to understand racism, let alone do what needs to be done to end it. And it's more than that, too. It's propaganda. It's white supremacists saying, again, this is not our fault, the real problem here is your unwillingness to forget.

9/11? Never forget.

The Holocaust? Never forget.

400 years of rape and murder and enslavement of an entire race, followed by 140-plus years of pretty much the same stuff, much of which is still happening right this very second? Forget. Now, motherfuckers!!! Forget!!

5 Tips For Slightly Less Dysfunctional QPOC Community

Originally published February 2012

Queer POC community can be severely dysfunctional. That's true of all kinds of community, really, but in queer communities dysfunction can reach an exceptionally high level of holy shit. To help with this, I've compiled this short list of things we can all do to kick the dysfunction down a notch.

Don't Take Sides When You Really Have No Idea What's Going On

Unless you were there and saw and heard everything that happened, you don't *know* anything. Just because one of the people in a disagreement is your friend doesn't mean that person is right (or innocent). Loyalty is important, but try to be loyal to your friends without making judgments about people who have issues with your friends.

Chill. You Are Not the Queer Behavior Police

Queer POC community is, I think, at least in part, about reject-ing mainstream (heteronormative, sexist, racist, homophobic, etc.) social systems that don't help people feel free. Still, often, we mimic those same busted systems when navigating our own communities and relationships. What this often ends up look-ing like is queers telling other queers how to do queerness: what to wear, who to date, what to read, what to think, in order to be authentically queer. In other words, "Here are the boxes you must fit into in order to avoid fitting into boxes." Y'all see the problem here, right? Stop. That's ridiculous.

Don't Be A Self-Righteous Dick

The bible says, do unto others as you would have them do unto you. And then it goes on to condone lots of rape and killing. So, it's mostly bullshit. Still, the initial idea is a good one. Translation: Don't be a dick. Don't be unkind to people who have not been unkind to you. Don't talk shit about people who don't talk shit about you. (You could even take it a step further and not talk shit about people who *do* talk shit about you, but, hey, you gotta walk before you can run, right?) We all have our triggers. We all have past hurts. But they do not give us license to be reckless, thoughtless, trauma-monsters raining down self-righteous asshole-ness under the heading of, "I must do whatever I have to do to feel safe!" If feeling safe requires unfortunately high levels of dickishness on your part, consider tweaking your coping mechanisms.

Stop Saving Face

This is good advice in QPOC community and everywhere else. Because we are so often led around by our egos, we often put a lot of energy into saving face. Rejection is hard, but it's a necessary part of life and if we accept and even embrace it, it can help us grow. But if we always respond to rejection by pretending we didn't care anyway (As in: I just got fired, but I really didn't want that job anyway and I was totally thinking about quitting because they're kinda racist and stuff; or, I just got dumped but I didn't really like that person anyhow and I was planning on breaking up with them), then we really don't get to take advantage of what rejection offers us—an opportunity to really consider what we might have done that didn't work, so that we can avoid making the same mistakes over and over again. It's not always somebody else's fault. It's not always somebody else's loss. Sometimes it's you. Sometimes it's your loss. Saving face and letting your ego dictate how you respond to rejection only muddies the waters of self-reflection.

Hold Your Homies Accountable

Again, just because someone is your friend doesn't mean they're right. In fact, just because someone is your friend doesn't mean they don't sometimes do extremely fucked-up shit. If you know that your friends are doing fucked-up shit, call them out. Hold them accountable. They don't get a pass to act a fool and hurt people because y'all grew up together, or they saved your life that time you almost choked on your In 'N Out burger, or even because they are always there for you. And being "neutral" in the face of your friends' bad behavior can be tantamount to condoning it. So, don't. Hold your friends accountable, and give them room to do the same for you.

Together, we can end QPOC community dysfunction in our lifetimes!

Whack Jobs Are Not the Problem (You Are)

Originally published July 2012

A couple of weeks ago, I wrote a post about why I don't talk to strange white people about race. Basically, what it boils down to is that those conversations are too unpredictable (or, too predictable, maybe), can be scary, and are almost always pointless. Most of the response to the post was very positive. But one response that really sticks out in my mind is:

"I'm a strange white girl but I get it. There are plenty of whack jobs on this planet, and we're not going to convert them any time soon. I've wasted enough time and energy on them myself to know by now it's not worth it. All so well said BGD!!!"

Hmm.

First of all, I never suggested that white people not enter into conversations about race with other white people. In fact, I explicitly say that white people should be the ones taking that on. So, she's already washing her hands of any responsibility. Okay. Still, she is making some attempt (however half-assed) to understand. She is trying to show some amount of solidarity. Notice how she uses the word *we*. As if we are the same (we're not). She really wants me to know that she *gets it*.

Only she doesn't.

She really doesn't.

Because racism isn't really about "whack jobs" at all.

Racism isn't crazy motherfuckers in white hoods. It isn't cowards slinging racial slurs from behind anonymous keyboards. I mean, it is. But it is so, so much more than that. Really, if racism were just those things, just whack jobs, it wouldn't be nearly the force in this world that it is.

Racism is, in reality, a huge, systemic, deeply-rooted plague that exists everywhere and affects everything, that degrades and starves and rapes and murders people without losing its breath. It is built on hundreds of years of oppression and genocide. It is in our government, in our entertainment, in our literature, in our corporations, in our language. This entire country was *built on it*. It is everywhere, and it is insidious and subtle just as often as it is open and obvious.

It is not that crazy dude *over there*.

I see the appeal to white folks in thinking about racism this way. The "whack job" approach allows people to separate racist thinking and behavior from themselves. It's that crazy screaming dude over there who's racist. It's your drunk uncles. It's your he-was-so-quiet-and-seemed-so-normal-before-he-walked-into-the-mall-and-started-shooting-people   neighbors. All of whom you can shake your heads at with furrowed brows while proclaiming that you're "not like that."

But you *are*.

White people, you need to get this: you *are* racist. You uphold white supremacy in big and small ways every day, whether you mean to or not. The first step is admitting that you are part of the problem.

If you want to understand how and why, read a book. Read a hundred books. Take a workshop. Read as many books and take as many workshops as you need to be able to stop pretending it's other white people and *not you*.

Trust me. It's you.

Resistance Is the Secret Of Queer Joy

Originally published May 2012

I've said it before: it's hard being a black woman in the world. It's hard being any kind of black person. Any kind of woman. Add queerness to the mix, and life becomes an amazing kind of struggle, one filled with enormous losses and small triumphs.

The triumphs, however small, are always significant. I'm not talking about huge social justice movements, but rather the smaller things that always spark those movements, the smaller things that keep those movements going. I'm talking about black women, domestic workers, refusing to give up their seats on buses in Montgomery, Alabama. Not just Rosa Parks, but all the women who refused to get up before her. Each of their actions was a small triumph. Even when they got arrested, which they did. Because the small triumph wasn't in the outcome, but in the act of resistance itself.

During the Stonewall Riots of 1969, when some of Greenwich Village's most marginalized queers—homeless youth, trans women, drag queens—fought back against police brutality, every brick thrown, every foot of ground held, was a small triumph. When the police grabbed folk singer Dave Van Ronk—who had heard the commotion from a bar two doors away from the Stonewall and come to help—he didn't run. He wasn't gay, but he had experienced police violence during antiwar demonstrations. He said: "As far as I was concerned, anybody who'd stand against the cops was all right with me, and that's why I stayed in." His fighting, his allyship, was a small triumph.

Alice Walker wrote that resistance is the secret of joy. I think this is true for people of color, for queers, for all of us whose lives are deemed less valuable in a hateful world run by evil people. Resistance comes in many, many forms. It comes in the throwing of bricks, but not only in the throwing of bricks. It comes, most often, in quieter, less media-worthy ways.

When I was a kid, I was forced to go to church on Sundays. Much of it was boring and terrible, and as soon as I was old enough to refuse to go, I did. Not all of it was terrible, though. One thing that was wonderful was that, always, at some point during the sermon, we would all be instructed by the pastor to turn to the person next to us and say, "God loves you and so do I." All these years later, I don't know about the *God loves you* part. But the *And so do I* was surely an act of resistance. The pastor knew—we all knew—that the world did not love us.

We all knew that loving each other as hard as we could was how we survived in a world that wanted to kill us, and that made our love an act of defiance.

Little did the pastor know that the girl who recited elaborate bible verses so beautifully would grow up to be a radical, feminist, pussy-licking queer. Yet my love for my community is the same kind of love we promised each other in church every Sunday.

One morning, a couple of weeks ago, I awoke to a terrible pain in my shoulder. I injured it a few years ago and it gives me trouble ever since. This one morning, I needed to be at my computer, writing things for y'all, and I knew my shoulder wasn't going to let me do it. So, I texted my friendly QTPOC massage therapist and asked if she could squeeze me in last minute. She did, and my shoulder, my whole body, was much happier for it. That was an act of resistance. On my part and hers. Her love for and investment in the wellness of queer people of color is an amazing act of resistance, and so is my investment in my own wellness.

I created this blog as an act of resistance. I created it as a way to reclaim the idea of dangerousness in a world that insists that as a black woman I am scary and aggressive and angry by default (I am angry, but it is not by default). I created this blog as a safe space for queer women of color who are tired of holding their tongues so as not to offend non-queer people of color, and white people, queer and not queer. And every time I post something here, something that is meant to inform or nurture my community, I get push-back from men and white people who want to tell me and all of us that we should *shut the fuck up*, that what we have to say has *no value*. I delete those comments so that the people I am creating safe space for don't have to see them, don't have to have yet another experience of being hated, because we get that enough everywhere else. But I know that hatred is there. I do this anyway. It is my every-day act of resistance.

For me, this blog is a small triumph. This blog is how I love my community, how all the writers featured here love ourselves and our people, of which, if you are reading this and recognizing your experience at all, you might be one. This entire endeavor is a love letter to you. It is my way, our way, of pushing back.

My childhood pastor was onto something. Turning to each other and naming our love is a radical and important act. Loving other queers, other people of color, and other queers of color especially, *is* an act of resistance. Loving us in all the ways I do, including fucking us, is about more than just sex or even friendship. The intentional act of loving other brown queers is about healing, in a world that says we are not worthy, that things like pleasure and care and security and unconditional love are not for us.

It's not true, my loves, my lovers. *They are for us.* Give me your hand. Let me show you how much they are for us.

10 Things Us Queers (And the Rest of Y'all) Can Do Today to Grow A Little

Originally published May 2012

I think I'm a pretty self-reflective person. I think I try really hard to listen and learn and grow. I like the idea of evolving. Some days I evolve more than other days. Some days I do the opposite of evolving. Which, I guess, is still evolving, but in less desirable ways.

The hard work of self-reflection and emotional evolution are everyday practices. Every day, there are things I can do to grow, even if just a little bit. Doing these things won't make me perfect. Nothing will ever make me perfect. But I can grow to be better at this human being thing. Here are some ways I know that may be helpful to you:

1. **Stop hiding behind your intellect.** Or your philosophy of life. Or your spiritual practice. Okay, so you're smart enough to win arguments with carefully constructed points. Okay, so

you learned a long time ago that you have to put yourself first. Okay, so you're a Buddhist. So what? You want a cookie? Nah. You fucked up, and you need to own it. When you gossip about people and call it *speaking your truth*, when you exhibit the same behaviors as people you claim to despise but somehow find ways to justify that behavior in yourself using skilled debate and footnotes, when you are adamant about showing love to the earth but terrible at showing it to other human beings, something aint right. You need to get on that.

2. Accept that racism/ sexism/ heterosexism/ transphobia/ ableism and all sorts of other really effed up stuff exists in the world. That we're not making it up. And then accept that you are either part of the solution, or part of the problem. If you can't list any concrete ways in which you are part of the solution (and, for the record, "Some of my best friends are black," is not going to cut it), accept that you are part of the problem. And get on changing that.

3. **Embrace your wrongness.** Being wrong, knowing it, and holding that knowledge can be really powerful. Once you know you're wrong, you can give up trying to win that argument and actually put your energy into listening, and maybe even learning something. Only dickheads and Republicans put energy into winning arguments when they know they're

wrong. Are you a dickhead? Are you a Republican?? What the fuck are you doing on this blog?!

4. Which leads me to...**Give up being right.** I have a friend who I kicked it with a lot a several years ago who would have an argument with someone (sometimes me) and get so wrapped up in how right she was that the friendship would suffer, and sometimes even end, because she couldn't bear not having her rightness be acknowledged. She lost a lot of friends this way. The truth is, sometimes, you can be right *or* you can be friends. If you have to choose between the two, and your friendship means enough to you to be worth keeping, then there's only one choice that makes sense. So get over yourself. K?

5. **Take an emotional risk.** I have known people who, in all the time I have spent with them, have never once taken an emotional risk. You know, people who only ask questions whose answers they already know so they don't run the risk of being hurt by truths they can't handle. Or people who never say I love you first. Or people who never say the thing that is at the back of their tongues, the thing that they are afraid will make them more vulnerable than they have ever been. I have been this person myself at times. Honestly, I have been this person many, many times. But I work on it every day.

6. **Hold hands with someone.** I think holding hands is one of the most vulnerable and connected things you can do with another person. Sometimes, if you lace your fingers with theirs, you can feel someone's pulse in their hands. Go ahead. Feel someone's pulse. Let them feel yours. It can be seriously liberating.

7. **Create a boundary/respect a boundary.** Creating boundaries is one way to let people know what you need. Respecting other people's boundaries is one way to meet another person's needs. The two go hand in hand. If you're dynamite about setting boundaries and lax about respecting the boundaries of others, or vice versa, something's off. I will admit that I have never been terrific at either of these things. But I'm much better than I used to be, and I'm working hard on both. What I'm working hardest on is understanding for myself the boundaries I'm setting and why I am setting them, where those needs are coming from, if they are real or just a way of controlling relationships and having the upper hand. If I'm just trying to get my way, without any regard for the needs of the people I claim to care about, that's not real boundary-setting. That's douchebaggery.

8. **Separate what happened from your story about what happened.** When I was six, I had the lead in my 2nd-grade class play and my mother didn't come to the show. I was dev-

astated and, as a six-year-old, I thought it meant that my mother didn't love me enough. I grew up believing that. It became my story about my mother. Every time my mother did anything to disappoint me, every time she failed to show up in any way, it added truth to my story. Only it wasn't truth. It was never truth. It was a story created by a wounded six-year-old. It took me 25 years to realize that. When I did, my life, my way of thinking about my mother and myself, my way of relating to everyone in my life changed. It didn't make me perfect. I still behave sometimes in response to that story, with my mother and with everyone, but A LOT less than I used to. And when I do, I know what's actually happening, I know it's that story and not something real.

9. **Check your ego.** My ego is enormous, and I come ego-first into most difficult interactions. I used to think that my ego was there to protect me from things like rejection. But at some point I realized that it's really there to protect *itself* from rejection. If in protecting itself it also happens to protect me, cool. But if what I need is different from what my ego needs, I'm fucked. Because my ego doesn't really give a shit about what I need. That's why it's so necessary for me to put that bitch (my ego) in check. If we are constantly being protected from rejection, we miss out on a lot of life's really important lessons.

10. **Say you're sorry.** There's someone out there who you wronged. You know it. You did effed up things, said really mean shit, lied, cheated, whatever. And you never apologized.

At some point, you started regretting it. But you felt so much guilt, or so much time had passed, that you weren't sure if you should go there, if you should bring it up again. Well, you should. If you want people to say they're sorry when they hurt you, you better damn well be someone who says you're sorry when you hurt other people. It's not really that complicated.

How To Know
If You Are White

Originally published October 2012

When I talk about "white people" I am talking about people who exist in bodies that give them access to white privilege. Some people exist in these bodies and get these privileges but don't ID as white. The thing about whiteness, though, is that you don't have to claim it to have it. You may not want to be white, for whatever reasons, but you don't choose whiteness. Whiteness chooses you. And when it does, it gives you— whether you want or acknowledge them or not—a whole slew of privileges that non-white folks don't get. Even if you are poor. Even if you are a woman. Even if you are queer and/or trans. Even if you are elderly. Even if you are a person with a disability. All of these things will, of course, affect your life in enormous ways and affect your access to any number of things. But they don't erase whiteness.

So, if you're confused about whether or not whiteness has chosen you, here's a few questions to help you sort it out.

How to Know If You Are White:

1. Do you look white? If this seems in any way like a complicated question, it can be easily discerned by walking into a fancy store (in clean, neat clothing) and seeing how the people who work there treat you. Do you get dirty looks upon entering? Do the shopkeepers glance at each other with worry? Do you notice people following you around to make sure you're not stealing anything? If not, you may be white.

2. When you are walking down the street and a cop car rolls by, do you feel safer because the police are around? Because they are there to protect you should something go wrong? If so, you may be white.

3. Do people ask you where you're from, and when you answer, "I'm from here," do they ask, "No, like, where are you *from* from?" If not, you may be white.

4. Are people visibly surprised when you are smart and articulate? If not, you may be white.

5. Have you ever been mistaken for a valet while wearing a suit? If not, you may be white.

6. Does the idea of driving through Mississippi fill you with apprehension? If not, you may be white.

7. Do people reach out and touch your hair/body without your permission and then accuse you of being too sensitive or of overreacting when you don't like it? If not, you may be white.

8. Do you regularly experience racism (note: racism is a system in which people are given less access to employment, education, safe and adequate housing, legal representation, etc. based on their race; racism is not people "not liking you" because of your race). If not, you may be white.

9. Do you see a lot of people who are the same color as you in movies, on TV, in magazines, etc. who are not portraying stereotypes or caricatures? If so, you may be white.

10. When you stand up for yourself, do people accuse you of being too angry? If not, you may be white.

11. Do people assume, without knowing you or ever speaking to you, that you are unintelligent, a criminal, good with computers, a terrorist, lazy, that you don't speak English, or that you are poor? If not, you may be white.

Hope this helps!

9 Queers Who Won't Survive the Apocalypse

Originally published August 2012

The Apocalypse will be here in a few short months, and I've started to realize that some of the queers I know will never survive it. It makes me sad, but...hey, more brains for zombie me! To give y'all a heads up, so you're not surprised when your friends start disappearing, I've compiled this handy list:

1. That white girl with the blunt asymmetric haircut and the supervisory NPIC job who always cries and tells you how poor she grew up when you call her out on her racism. She will likely be killed by zombies eating off her face to get to her tear ducts because, to zombies, white girl tears taste like honey dew melon and sex.

2. That performance artist with the crushing need to be the center of attention at all times. If you can't blend in during the Apocalypse, you're fucked. The rabid wild dogs will get you first.

3. That perpetually-frowning queer who, every time you ask him in passing how he's doing, launches into a long, drawn out, half hour long story about his chihuahua's bad breath and the outrageous prices of organic dog mouthwash, or how his ex is committing a heinous dating etiquette foul by going out with someone who he himself used to crush on (which is not a foul at all), or how his mom keeps looking at him as though she suspects he is a gay and how it's giving him insomnia and irregular periods. He will probably be killed by organ thieves who, while he is distracted by the sounds of his own voice, take his liver.

4. That way too happy motherfucker whose compulsive positivity silences your truth. Like, when you say, "I'm so busy with all these jobs and I don't get to sleep and I'm so tired and it's terrible," they say, "You mean, you're happy to have a job because a lot of people don't, right?" No, bitch, that's not what I meant! They will probably be burned up in the too-hot post-apocalypse sunshine. And they'll probably like it.

5. That white hipster who is always rocking that Che shirt. He will probably be punched through the guts by the ghost of Che Guevara. (I'm assuming there will be ghosts in the apocalypse. Right?)

6. That moody, annoying ass emo cancer who makes everything an emotional mini-drama. Um, I just asked you to pass me the mustard. It doesn't mean I don't think you're pretty. Also, it's the apocalypse, and nobody is all that pretty right now. No, that doesn't mean I'm checking out other girls! She will probably also be killed by zombies, who will get her while she is sobbing and listening to Fall Out Boy way too loudly to be able to hear them coming.

7. That 100-pound genderqueer who always gets mistaken for a seven-year old from behind because of all those neon-pink leg warmers, bedazzled headbands, and shiny plastic shoes. Way too easy to spot. He will probably be killed by a gang of seven year-olds who didn't mean to kill him but who, in the dreary grayness of the Apocalypse, got so excited to see colors again that they accidentally loved/ate him to death.

8. That white lesbian who owns the yoga studio. She will most certainly be killed by a roving band of Indian undead who resent her appropriating their culture and then making the classes too expensive for them and all their poor brown queer friends to attend. They will prob suffocate her with her own yoga mat.

9. That super-cute boi whose wide eyes, pretty brown skin, love of high-water pants, and shy demeanor remind you of a young Michael Jackson. They will be killed by zombie Mi-

chael Jackson (who looks exactly like regular Michael Jackson circa 2006), who, in death, finally realized the terrible effect that racism had on his pysche, and is mad now, and wants his original face back.

Read A Book! Or, Why I Don't Talk To Strange White Folks About Race

Originally published July 2012

L ast night I had a Facebook chat with a friend of mine who was feeling all stabby because a white woman she knows posted a ridiculous and offensive status message about race. This person, who, according to my friend, appropriates from at least five different cultures on a daily basis, is a thorn in my friend's side, but one she has to put up with to a certain extent for professional reasons. My friend was tempted to respond to this person's status message, but was hesitant because she didn't want to create drama in her professional life. She didn't exactly ask for my advice, but I gave it to her anyway. ***Don't bother.***

As socially and politically conscious people of color, we are constantly having to spend time and energy responding to the nonsense that so often spews forth from the mouths and keyboards of clueless white people. Someone writes something fucked up, and as tiring as the thought of it sometimes is, it's hard for us not to respond, not to check the idiot in question, not to try, at least, to make them hear sense. This desire comes from the fact that we, POC, have to live in this often-ridiculous world and we want to do whatever we can to make it less ridiculous, for our own sanity if nothing else. So, some melanin-challenged individual whose race analysis is about as solid as maple syrup writes something idiotic and we feel like we have to say *something*. We can't just let it go unchecked or unchallenged. So, we say something. And what happens?

What happens, most of the time, is *nothing good*. Why? Because the person who posted the thing that offended us did so because it's what they really think, it's what they actually believe, it's the conclusion that they have *somehow* come to after 25 or 30 or 40 years of living in this world. The ridiculous position they just laid down isn't something they just came up with. It's their fucking *philosophy*, and they mean that shit. And now here you come telling them, *uh uh, nope, your analysis is flawed and this is why*. And you're right. You really are. And guess what? *It doesn't matter*. Because one woman's incredibly offensive gibberish is another woman's ideology. Nothing you say is going to change that. But you might spend a lot of time and energy trying. Time and energy that could be much better spent on much better things. Much better things that don't get the time and energy they deserve and require because we are too busy being distracted by the lackadaisically ignorant.

I decided a few years ago that I would no longer talk to strange white people about race. By strange, I mean white people who are strangers to me. (And writing about race on this blog, which is a forum for QPOC, is not the same as engaging with white people about it). I decided, in fact, that unless they were people I knew well, people I trusted, the subject of race would be off-limits. With very few exceptions, I've stuck to that policy, and it's served me very well. I've saved a lot of energy this way. Often, when a white person who I do not trust tries to talk to me about race and I shut it down, the person in question says something like, "How will I know if you don't, like, teach me?" Or, even better, "You're not responding to my questions because you know you're wrong," as though my very carefully thought-out refusal to engage with them makes my analysis invalid. Hmm.

Listen. It's not my job to teach white people about race. If they want to have a better analysis on race, they can read a book. Shit, they can read *a thousand books*, because a thousand books have already been written on the subject. Films have been made, art installations have been erected. *It's all been said*. (And, really, if you're 35 and you haven't bothered to get educated on the subject yet, you can't really be all that interested, can you?) And if conscious white people would step it up and check their clueless race-mates on their shit, we POC wouldn't have to always be put in these positions.

More importantly, engaging with strange white people about race feels incredibly *unsafe*. If I do it anyway, because, after all, they just want to "understand" my position, then I am putting their need to "understand" ahead of my own need to protect my psychological and emotional well-being. *And why on earth should I do that?* Especially when the likelihood of that understanding actually happening is slim to none? And the likelihood that my position will be mocked, dismissed, or attacked is very high?

Nah, I'm cool.

In the end, my friend decided that it was better for her own sanity, for her own well-being, to not engage with this person. I think it was a good decision, and a decision we POC should allow ourselves, and each other, to make more often. We need to be able to walk away from these conversations when we know that nine out of ten times they will traumatize us, anger us, and exhaust us. And, unfortunately, give us absolutely nothing in return.

Afterthoughts:
Many people, if not most, have a really hard time with nuance, particularly when discussing issues such as racism. The point

of this piece is not to tell POC that talking to white people about race is "wrong" or "bad" or even that you "shouldn't" do it. That's way too simple. The point is to make room for POC to prioritize their own well-being over the "education" of white people, which I don't think we allow ourselves enough. White supremacy demands that we centralize whiteness at all times, even when we are supposed to be taking care of ourselves. I reject the idea that white people's education about my experiences of racism is more important than my psychological well-being and my right to say no to that kind of engagement. If other folks of color want to engage white people in these ways, that's their *choice*. I am making room for a different *choice* for people of color who don't want to put energy into white people's education.

I have had young POC ask, "If we don't educate them, how can there be change?"

First of all, a person of color making a decision not to engage or educate white people about race is in no way hindering white people from learning. As I wrote in this piece, thousands of books have already been written on these subjects. It's all been said already. White people have more access to education than anyone. If they want to learn, they can. The idea that the individual POC of their choice should stop everything and "teach" them is exactly what white privilege looks like.

Secondly, individual POC taking on the work of educating white people (and white "allyship" in general) is not the only way to create change (I'd argue it's not an effective way at all). Most of the people in the world are not white. If our movements need allies, it makes more sense to me to look to each other, to create solidarity across oppressed difference. What would it mean to actively teach young Asian Americans about anti-blackness? What would it mean to actively teach young black Americans about Native erasure? Doesn't it make more sense to put energy into creating coalition between marginalized groups who have common interests and overlapping experiences? I'd argue that this would be the most important and effective way of pushing back against oppression and creating change. But we seldom have energy or focus for that kind of building because we are told that the "education" of white people is all-important. I want us to challenge that idea.

The White-Skinned Elephant In the Room

Originally published August 2012

I have been thinking about this post for a long time. I have been ruminating on how, and whether, to say these things. I have been talking to trusted friends to get their thoughts and input. I have spoken to other writers about how to collaborate on a piece like this, so we could share the backlash that would surely come. It has been weeks and months of considering what, exactly, to say and how, exactly, to say it. Friends, other writers, have told me they are afraid to go where I am about to go. I have been a little afraid myself.

Our fear comes from the fact that no one seems to talk about this, at least not in an open forum. It also comes from the fact that identity politics are a serious bitch and people get hella touchy about them. As a result of this silence and this touchiness, there is big fat white-skinned elephant in the room.

Well. This is *Black Girl Dangerous*, and pointing out the elephant is sometimes what we have to do. So, here goes.

I'll start here:

In 2003, I moved to Denver. How and why isn't important, but I ended up there. I never really liked it, never felt at home there, but I was tired of moving, so I stayed. For the first few years, I couldn't find any community that felt like a fit for me. And then, in 2006, I discovered some queers of color, a whole group of them, a small but significant community. I was thrilled. I started hanging out with folks, and one day I was invited to a gathering. It was a group started for QPOC to get together and talk about life, problems, to vent and get support or whatever. There were awesome people there, and I met many cool folks. But...something was a little strange.

There were one or two people there who, to my eyes, looked completely white. I'm talking blue-eyed, fair-skinned (not light-skinned, *white-skinned*) people. These people were not calling themselves allies. They were calling themselves POC. I was...confused. I looked around at the other POC there, and none of them seemed perturbed about it.

In all my life on the East Coast, I had never encountered this. Where I come from, people of color are people who walk through the world in skin that gets hella bullshit brought down on them. Because their skin is not white, their lives are more difficult. They are discriminated against in employment and housing. They are profiled by police. They are followed around in stores (in the case of black and brown people) because they are marked as thieves. The list of bullshit they have to deal with goes on and on.

But here, in Denver, were these white-skinned, sometimes blue-eyed people, who I could not imagine having ever experienced any of that, calling themselves POC and talking mad shit about "white people". And it wasn't only the one or two at that first gathering. As I spent more and more time in that community in Denver, I was introduced to more and more people who looked white but called themselves POC.

What I discovered was that these people usually had POC ancestry. More often than not, a grandparent, or even great-grandparent, who was a person of color. And because of this, because of their brown ancestors, they called themselves POC, even though they themselves presented as white. And not only did they call themselves POC, but they very strongly, adamantly, separated themselves from the idea of whiteness. And I was like...really?

Again, none of the other visible people of color seemed to have any problem with this. The other visible people of color even dated these white-skinned people and described themselves as being in QPOC relationships. Everyone else was so mum about it, in fact, that I, new to this community, felt completely intimidated about bringing it up, about asking why and how these folks were people of color. So, I never did.

When I went back to the East Coast, the issue became some-what moot, at least in my immediate vicinity. In Philly, the queer POC community I knew were all visible people of color. The only people I knew who weren't were from other places, and they were still few. So, it kinda fell off my radar.

And then I started hanging out in Oakland.

Where, once again, I encountered people whose skin is white and who identify as people of color. And not only identify, but OWN that shit. People who, with their white skin, lead work-shops and arts organizations and panels about being POC.

I'm not gonna lie. I'm feeling some type of way about this.

As a visible person of color, as a woman who walks around in this very brown skin, with this kinky hair and these features, all of which invite discrimination, degradation, and presupposi-tions based on race into my life *every day*, it has been hard (and is becoming impossible) for me to continue to be quiet about this. The idea that some people (white-skinned people) get to have all the benefits of whiteness and *still* claim owner-ship of POC-ness, without anyone raising an eyebrow, is, to me, problematic.

Let me say here that there are people I like and love who fall into this category: white-skinned people who call themselves POC. This post is not meant to hurt them. It is also not meant to be skin-policing. What it is meant to do is start a conversa-tion. A conversation that I just don't see happening anywhere else. It's a complicated conversation, and undoubtedly a difficult one. But I believe it needs to be had.

So, this is the first in what I hope will be a series of posts, by me and by other contributors, about white-skin privilege in POC community* and what it means, in reality, to be a person of color who has to deal with racism directed at oneself, as opposed to being a white-skinned person with POC ancestry who does not. Can you really have white skin and *be* a person of color? *Does that even make sense?* Or is this yet another way that whiteness gets to have its way, gets to be whatever it chooses, even if it chooses to be *not white*.

There it is. I said it. I got it out and I feel better already.

So...let's talk?

Afterthoughts:

This post rubbed "white-presenting POC" the wrong way. To say the least. People who get all the benefits of whiteness but who claim "POC" really did not appreciate me questioning them on that and felt extremely offended at the idea of having a conversation about their privilege. Their reaction made me even more certain that these conversations need to be happening.

The term "of color" was first created in 1977 during the National Women's Conference in Houston. A group called "Black

Women's Agenda" came to the conference with a Black women's plan of action that they wanted to be included in the conference's proposed plan. The other "minority" women at the conference saw this and wanted to be included in the Black women's agenda. The group agreed, but obviously they had to change the name. This is how "women of color" came about. It came about as a way for racialized women whose experiences of oppression were overlapping to organize together under a common term that took into account both their shared experiences and how those experiences were different from the experiences of white women. Once the term "women of color" caught on, "people of color" followed.

Understanding the history of the term, I find it amazing that anyone who doesn't have an experience of racialized oppression would use it.

Since I wrote this piece, though, my thinking around this topic has changed. In particular, my concern about who is using the term "POC" and why has given way to a feeling of some indifference. I still very much believe that because the term was created by and for people who are racially oppressed, to mark a common experience of marginalization, it belongs to us and should not be used by people who don't have that experience. However, I understand now that the term has been co-opted to a point of no return. At this point, I think it makes a lot more sense to coin a new term, or bring into more popular usage an already-existing term, for those of us who do experience racialized oppression, so that we can continue to talk about our shared and diverse experiences without being expected to make room for white privilege.

The Thing About Being A Little Black Girl In the World: For Quvenzhané Wallis

Originally published February 2013

The thing about being a little black girl in the world is that even when you are the youngest person ever to be nominated for an Academy Award, many people will use the occasion not to hold you up for all of the amazing things you obviously are, but to tear you down for the ways you don't look like them, the ways your name isn't their kind of right, the ways you don't remind them of themselves, the ways you are not blonde or blue-eyed, as if those things could possibly matter when set against the otherwordly talent and beauty and brilliance you possess.

The thing about being a little black girl in the world is that you come into it already expected to be less than you almost certainly are, the genius and radiant darkness you possess already set up to be overlooked, dismissed or erased by almost everyone you will ever meet.

The thing about being a little black girl in the world is that even when you are everything, some people will want you to be nothing. They will look at you through the nothing-colored glasses they will put on every time you enter a room. And the bigness of you, the outstandingness, the giftedness, will be invisible to them.

The thing about being a little black girl in the world who is already, at nine years old, confident enough to demand that lazy, disrespectful reporters call you by your name, is that most people will not understand the amount of comfort in one's own skin it takes to do that, will not be able to grasp the sheer fierceness of it, the boldness, the certainty, the love for yourself, and will not be blown away at seeing you do it, though they should be.

The thing about being a little black girl in the world is that your right to be a child, to be small and innocent and protected, will be ignored and you will be seen as a tiny adult, a tiny black adult, and as such will be susceptible to all the offenses that people two and three and four times your age are expected to endure.

But take heart.

Because the thing about being a little black girl in the world is that you are descended from people whose incredible strength and resilience are alive and kicking in you.

The thing about being a little black girl in the world is that you are made from beauty and struggle and soul.

The thing about being a little black girl in the world is that when you have talent, you probably have more of it in your tiniest toe than most of the people who tear you down have in their entire families.

The thing about being a little black girl in the world is that if you are lucky enough to know your own worth, you know everything you need to know.

The thing about being a little black girl in the world is that you will be surrounded by other black girls who know. And they will hold your hand and braid your hair and laugh with you. They will tell you that you are a gift. They will let you be perfect and let you be flawed. They will rock you in their arms and protect your heart. They will whisper and shout about all that you are. And in a world that wants you gone from the very moment you are born, they will help you stay alive. Some of them will even help you get free.

We got you, girl. With so much love.

Afterthoughts:

This post was written in response to the treatment 9-year-old Academy Award nominee Quvenzhané Wallis received at the Oscars. Namely, that white reporters refused to call her by her name, because they couldn't be bothered to learn how to say it, that the host of the show made sexualized comments about the child, and that *The Onion* called her a cunt as a 'joke'. When it was published, this became our most popular post ever, read by hundreds of thousands of people worldwide. The response was overwhelmingly positive. In a radio interview I did about the piece, I was asked whether I knew if Quvenzhané Wallis had seen it. I did not know, but it doesn't really matter because, although what happened to Quvenzhané inspired the post in the moment, it's really for and about every little black girl who has ever been denied the right to shine in the fullness of her brilliance and humanity.

On Getting Free

Originally published February 2013

A long time ago, when you were a wee thing, you learned something, some way to cope, something that, if you did it, would help you survive. It wasn't the healthiest thing, it wasn't gonna get you free, but it was gonna keep you alive. You learned it, at five or six, and it worked, it *did* help you survive. You carried it with you all your life, used it whenever you needed it. It got you out–out of your assbackwards town, away from an abuser, out of range of your mother's un-love. Or whatever. It worked for you. You're still here now partly because of this thing that you learned. The thing is, though, at some point you stopped needing it. At some point, you got far enough away, surrounded yourself with people who love you. You survived. And because you survived, you now had a shot at more than just staying alive. You had a shot now at getting free. But that thing that you learned when you were five was not then and is not now designed to help you be free. It is designed only to help you survive. And, in fact, it keeps you from being free. You need to figure out what this thing is and work your ass off to un-learn it. Because the things we learn to do to survive at all costs are not the things that will help us get FREE. Getting free is a whole different journey altogether.

Hey, White Liberals: A Word on the Boston Bombings, the Suffering of White Children, And the Erosion of Empathy

Originally published April 2013

H ey, White Liberals:

I needed to break protocol to reach out to you and let you know that you're killing me. No, worse. Much worse. You're robbing me of part of my humanity.

In lots of ways, really, and frequently, but right now let's just talk about this one way:

Your constant prioritization of the lives of white people over the lives of people of color is taking a serious toll on my psyche and those of many in my community. And by that I don't mean what you might expect. Most of us already know that racism and its BFF white supremacy have detrimental effects on people of color. Racial oppression leads to any number of unhealthy conditions, including high blood pressure, depression, heart disease, diabetes, and even asthma. But what I'm talking about is something different. Something I'm going to call DSWP: desensitization to the suffering of white people.

A few days ago, I was having lunch with a good friend who is Korean-American, and she told me that when she heard about the bombings at the Boston Marathon—the marathon itself being something she knew nothing about and immediately associated with white people—she found that she had a hard time...well, *caring*. I'm sure that sounds shocking to many people. But it didn't shock me. Because I was having the same feelings myself.

I really noticed it a few months back, during coverage of the Sandy Hook elementary school shootings. As news outlet after news outlet flashed photograph after photograph of mostly white children across TV screens and computer screens alike, I felt something I hadn't remembered ever feeling before upon hearing of the brutal murder of children: I felt numb. Not numb in the way that people in shock feel numb. Not numb because of the great weight of what had happened. This was a different kind of numbness.

I couldn't help but think about Trayvon Martin. He wasn't an elementary school kid when he was shot and killed by a racist with a gun, but he *was* just a 17-year-old boy, unarmed, walking down the street with a bag of Skittles. I thought of countless other Black youth who have been murdered by crazed gunmen with badges and police uniforms in the last few years. I also thought about the hundreds of brown children in Iraq and Afghanistan and Pakistan who have been killed by US forces on the ground and by drone strikes. I thought about how many times I didn't see any of their faces, smiling and innocent, splashed across the TV or the internet for days and weeks on end. I thought about how white people I know *weren't* posting links to stories about *those* children and what had happened to them. That they weren't writing Facebook statuses about how unbearable those kids' deaths were. And, seeing pictures of those little blonde children—because the blonde ones are always featured most prominently—I felt numb.

And it wasn't just me. The same was true for many of my majority-POC friends and many people in my community. Many of us seemed unable to feel what a person should be able to feel when another person, especially a child, has their life taken away. After all, we had always been able to feel it before. I thought about the numbness of my friends and about my own lack of connection, and I wondered what was happening to us. I didn't wonder for long, though, because the answer is really simple: *you* are happening to us, white liberals.

It shouldn't have to be this way. While many white people may not be capable of connecting emotionally to the humanity of people of color, we POC have always been capable of connecting to yours. Because all our lives we are told white people's stories—through news, television, movies, etc.—our ability to see white people as *people* has been pretty solid. (This is also probably due to the fact that we have never needed an excuse to kidnap, enslave, or mass murder you, which is always easier to do to a race of people when you can deny their humanity). But even in the face of all the evil that white people have perpetrated against us, most of us, in the face of some individual white person or small group of white people in pain or suffering, have still been able to feel compassion. Sympathy. Empathy. But lately...it's getting more and more difficult to feel those things.

Some of it has to do with the fact that the wars and subsequent occupations of Iraq and Afghanistan have gone on for more than a dozen years. For many of the younger folks I know, that's the better part of their entire lives. It's a whole third of mine. For a dozen years we have watched as the mainstream media has ignored the deaths of so many brown children, day after year after decade. I mean, they were ignoring the deaths of Black children all over the world, including here, way before that, but we didn't have to see them ignoring it so blatantly every morning and afternoon and evening and night on TV (that 24-hour news cycle is a bitch; they have time for everything except our stories). Also, before the internet, and specifically before bloggers, the killing of black children by police officers had much less chance of even being known about outside of the community in which it happened. So, you know, you could at least feign ignorance. But now we know how often these things are happening. And we know how often white people don't have a damn thing to say about it.

This is also true when it comes to the disappearances of black and brown women and children, which are all but ignored in the mainstream media. When our children go missing, there's barely a teardrop in the news cycle. When white children go missing, it's a national event.

Why don't our children get to be children? Why don't they ever get to be innocent?

What all this has resulted in is the displacement of compassion and empathy with anger and resentment. Because when the names of slain white children are spoken, I can barely hear them anymore. My ears are plugged with the unuttered names of the Black and brown children whose lives didn't mean enough to be spoken aloud on CNN. When I see photos of their smiling white faces, I can only imagine the smiles of fallen Black and brown children whose faces never grace the news.

I feel as if something important, something essential to my humanity, is being drained away every time you ignore the suffering and death of people who look like me and my family and my friends and my community, while devoting endless hours of attention to the suffering of people who look like you. Each time, I feel little less...well, I *feel a little less*.

And I'm not happy about it. I don't feel good about it. I don't want to be someone who can't empathize with people who don't look like me.

The only way to stop this is for you to stop ignoring our lives and our deaths and our stories. For you to put the names and faces of those Black and brown children in your news and on your Facebook pages. It is not enough for you to say, when confronted, that you care. You need to act like it. Because a part of our humanity—our empathy—is eroding. And that's not a good thing for any of us.

Afterthoughts:

Many white people had a hard time with this piece, as you might imagine. There was some outrage at the idea that I could dare not feel devastated about their children's suffering. That I, as a black person, would have the audacity to not burst into tears every time a white child is hurt, really angered some white folks. That was the tone of it. Basically: a black person, as less than a white person, is naturally obligated to care about the lives of white people no matter what. Not surprisingly, the white people who took issue never seemed to notice any of the stuff I wrote about the black and brown children whose deaths were getting no press. That still didn't bother them much. Their feeling seemed to be: *we don't need to care about your chil-*

dren, but you are a monster if you don't care about ours. Go figure.

An Open Love Letter
To Folks of Color

Originally published April 2012

D ear Fellow Folks of Color,

I am writing to tell you that I'm in love with you. I would have said it to your faces, but I don't have that kind of travel money.

What I love about you, POC, is…well, there's a lot.

First of all, I love that, despite what you may have heard, your ancestors pretty much built or invented everything that was ever built or invented in the world. They built the pyramids. They built the United States (this includes buildings, roads, bridges, and the entire economic system that came from the cotton of the South and which made this country a world power). They invented chess, jewelry, sculpture, dance. Air conditioning, the fire extinguisher. Guitars, horseshoes, rock and roll, mailboxes, motors, refrigerators, traffic lights. They invented chopsticks, spoons, *and* forks. To eat the food whose domestication they originated: rice, chocolate, potatoes, carrots, coffee, wheat, ice cream. I could go on. The first game of soccer was played by them. The first songs sung with the human voice were sung by them. By you. I mean, how could I *not* love you? (Also, I'm pretty sure you invented love.)

But that's really not even the half of it. POC, I love you because you are fierce. Because you are strong. Because you are hella resilient. Because despite living in a country that finds some new way every single day to tell you that you are less, you somehow continue to be more and more and more. Despite racism and xenophobia and poverty and white women's tears and Mitt Romney, you still manage, somehow, to hold it together. Even though the hero "Prince of Persia" is played by Jake Gyllenhaal; even though some people think "reverse racism" is a real thing; even though API folks are like .003% of the characters on US TV shows right now and most of them are on *Glee*, you haven't just given up and started speaking gibberish and throwing your feces. Which, under the circumstances, would be really understandable. No, instead you find more and more ways to survive, and not only to survive, but to thrive. Despite your children being gunned down by cops like every single day, despite your sisters dying in the heat of the desert while "sneaking" into a land that belongs to your own ancestors—not to mention being deported from that same land in record numbers—despite the CONSTANT beatings inflicted on your souls, you somehow still *have* souls. That's fucking amazing. I mean, I'm not surprised. Your ancestors couldn't have survived slavery and internment and genocide without some damn serious sturdy genes. But still. It's impressive.

I love you for all of these things.

I love you, too, for the way, despite all of this, you continue to love each other. I love you for knowing what community really is. I love you for understanding what family means. I love you for the way you lean into each other when you laugh, the way you rock when you hug, the way you cook and fight and die for each other. The way you forgive. The way you remember.

I love your thick lips and your thick/curly/kinky/bone-straight hair. I love your slanted eyes, and your round and not-round asses, and your high cheekbones and your big/tiny feet. I love your brown eyes. I LOVE your brown skin.

I love the way you do math (which you also invented), the way you dance, the way you talk. I love your fire. I love your anger.

Folks of Color, I am so fucking in love with you. So in love with *us*.

Sigh.

Yours,
Mia

The Myth of Shared Womanhood and How It Perpetuates Inequality

Originally published May 2013

I've been thinking a lot about shared female identity. A lot of people seem to think that being born with female parts bonds you in some significant way to other people who are born with female parts. In order to get the most out of all that bonded-female-parts-ness, there are events and outings that welcome female-born people only, places where we can listen to the music "we" like and talk about our periods or something. It goes like this: "women" have a different experience in the world than "men" and therefore understand each other on some deep level and in some universal way because of that experience. While I agree, of course, with that first part, I find the last part really tricky.

I don't feel any universal connection with all people who are born with female parts. I'm not sure I know anyone who actually does, not when you really break it down. Because, despite what mainstream (white) feminism and tampon commercials

106

would have us believe, "shared" female experience isn't really all that "shared" at all.

Let's take for example a well-known issue that affects women–the issue of "equal pay." We've all heard the statistic: in the US, women make 77 cents for every dollar a man makes on average. That sucks. But it's not quite the shared experience it seems. A recent report by the National Partnership for Women & Families shows that black women only make 70 cents for every dollar a man makes on average, and only 64 cents compared to every dollar paid to a white, non-Hispanic man. And Latinas make only 55 cents for every dollar made by a white, non-Hispanic man. Well, damn. That 77 cents never looked so good.

Of course, it's not just economics. There are many ways in which factors such as race, sexuality, gender presentation, and (dis)ability make the "collective" experience of one group of women vastly different from that of another. According to RAINN (Rape, Abuse & Incest National Network), 91% of people who are raped in the US are women. So, rape is a universal issue for women, right? Of course. When you break it down, though, "universal" gets complicated. The rate of rape and attempted rape for white women is 17.7%. For American Indian/Alaskan women it's 34.1%. And women with disabilities are raped at a rate at least twice that of women overall. So, while "women" have a collective experience of being more vulnerable to rape, some women are a whole lot more vulnerable to it than others. While that first statistic is always used to suggest a shared female experience of the world, the statistics that follow it show that women's experiences aren't really all that shared. Or at least not equally shared. Not anywhere *near* equally.

Despite these and a hundred other examples, the myth of shared female experience prevails. Why? Well, the easy answer is that because "women" are so vulnerable to so many different injustices, even if that vulnerability is vastly different from one group to another, lumping us all in together gives us a louder voice and more power to change things. Even if that's true, the downside of all this lumping together is significant. Because it allows the people with the loudest voices within the group to always be dominating the conversation. And because those voices rarely, if ever, even understand the experiences of the less-heard members of the group, not only can they not speak for them (which they shouldn't be doing anyway), *they can rarely even understand the importance of making space for them to speak for themselves*.

This is why today's mainstream feminist movements are still so white, even though women of color are 36.3% of the women in this country. It's why, even though "marriage equality" is all over the news all the time, you rarely see lesbians of color, and you never see disabled lesbians or trans lesbians, on TV. Because the voice of the privileged majority, even within a presumed non-privileged group, doesn't end up raising the voices of the less-heard group; it usually just drowns them out. What you end up with is groups within groups that feel, and are, completely disconnected from one another. So is the case with women in this country. (This also describes queer community and people of color community as a whole, and QTPOC community specifically.)

Yet, the myth of shared female experience persists. It gets used by certain groups, including Michigan Women's Music Festival, to exclude trans women because they presumably don't have all the parts necessary to participate in this "universal" female experience that doesn't actually exist anyway. The idea that cis women who attend this festival have a shared experience of womanhood–an experience that stretches like a rainbow bridge across race, sexuality, (dis)ability and economic class–that is so certain that no one without a vagina could possibly understand any of it is, frankly, absurd.

As a black, queer, cis woman who was raised working class, I feel almost completely disconnected from the experiences of white, straight, trans women who were raised wealthy. And much more so from the experiences of white, straight, cis women who were raised middle-class. Put me in a room full of either of these groups of women and I wouldn't be able to get away fast enough. I'd feel *incredibly* out of place.

In fact, put me in a room full of black lesbians and I won't likely do a whole lot of bonding. A room full of queer black women nerd-types? Ok, now we're getting closer.

Here's a quick list of rooms full of people where I will likely bond, in order of best to worst.

1. Black queer women who are nerdy in bookish ways, regardless of economic class.
2. Other queer women of color who are nerdy in bookish ways, who are working class.
3. Other queer women of color who are nerdy in bookish ways, regardless of class.
4. Black women, regardless of class and sexuality, who are nerdy in bookish ways.
5. Other women of color, regardless of class and sexuality, who are nerdy in bookish ways.

You see how complicated this is already??? A room full of white women is going to be somewhere around number 1006. Seriously, a "room full" of white women of any sort is a room I'm going to leave really quickly, and probably only have stumbled into by accident while looking for the bathroom.

My point is, possession of vaginas in and of themselves are neither what define women nor what bond women to each other. Shared experiences of the world, which include experiences of race, sexuality, (dis)ability, economic class, any number of nuanced vulnerabilities, love of french fries, etc. is what bonds women to each other. And continuing to talk about "women" as this vagina-having-but-otherwise-unspecific group, rather than looking closer and breaking down the ways in which our specific experiences of the world are impacted by race, sexuality, etc., only perpetuates the inequalities we're supposed to be trying to eradicate.

4 Ways To Push Back Against Your Privilege

Originally published February 2014

I've often said that it's not enough to acknowledge your privilege. And, in fact, that acknowledging it is often little more than a chance to pat yourself on the back for being so "aware." What I find is that most of the time when people acknowledge their privilege, they feel really special about it, really important, really glad that something so significant just happened, and then they just go ahead and do whatever they wanted to do anyway, privilege firmly in place. The truth is that acknowledging your privilege means a whole lot of nothing much if you don't do anything to actively push back against it.

I understand, of course, that the vast majority of people don't even acknowledge their privilege in the first place. I'm not talking to them. I'm talking to those of us who do. If we do, then we need to understand that acknowledgement all by itself isn't enough. No matter how cathartic it *feels*.

So, what does pushing back against your privilege look like? Well, here are just a few ways it can look (note: none of these is easy; that doesn't mean you shouldn't try):

1. Relinquish Power

If you are in a position of power and you are able to recognize and acknowledge that at least part of the reason you are there is your (white, male, cisgendered, able-bodied, class, etc.) privilege, then pushing back against that privilege means sharing that power with, or sometimes relinquishing it to, the folks around you who have less privilege and therefore less power. I had a conversation recently with my friend about her terrible white woman boss who, when the women of color she supervises have strong feelings about the way things are being run, including *the hiring of more white people over POC*, pulls rank on them. Her "I understand your feelings but I am, you know, the boss and it's my job to..." nonsense is exactly what **not** pushing back against your privilege looks like. On the other hand, "I was hired to supervise y'all, but I don't want to perpetuate this type of effed-up power dynamic and also I recognize that y'all have a better understanding about why we should not hire another white man, so I'm going to go ahead and defer to y'all" is exactly what pushing back against your privilege *does* look like.

2. Just Don't Go

If you have access to something and you recognize that you have it partly because of privilege, opt out of it. If you're an able-bodied person and that retreat you really, really want to go on isn't wheelchair accessible, and the organizers of said retreat have been asked and supported in making a change and done nothing, and you realize how fucked up that is, *don't go*. It works the same for women-only events that exclude trans women. Don't go. Even if you really, really want to go because your, like, fave artist ever is gonna be there. *Especially then*. Pushing back against your privilege often requires sacrifice. Sacrifice is hard sometimes, homies. If not being a dick were easy, everybody would do it! Acknowledging that something is messed up doesn't mean anything if you still participate just because, dang, you really want to and stuff.

3. Shut up

This one is so, so important. If you are a person with a lot of privilege (i.e. a white, straight, able-bodied, class-privileged, cisgender male or any combination of two or more of those) and you call yourself being against oppression, then it should be part of your regular routine to sit the hell down and shut the eff up. If you can recognize that part of the reason your opinion, your voice, carries so much weight and importance is because you are a white man (or whatever combination is working for you), then pushing back against your privilege often looks like shutting your face. Now, of course, using your privilege to speak out against oppression is very important. But I'm not talking about that. I'm talking about chiming in, taking up space, adding your two cents, playing devil's advocate, etc. when 1) no one asked you, 2) the subject matter is outside your realm of experience (why do you even think you get to have an opinion about the lives of black women??), 3) anything you say is just going to cause more harm because your voice, in and of itself, is a reminder that *you always get to have a voice* and that voice usually drowns out the voices of others.

4. Be careful what identities you claim

If you're a cis dude who is only into women but you call yourself 'queer' because all your friends are queer and plus you kissed a guy once and also you feel more politically aligned with queer folks...rethink that. Consider how your privilege (and sense of entitlement) gives you access to claim identities even when your lived experience doesn't support it. The same goes for white-presenting people who claim POC but by their own admission don't experience oppression based on race. Just consider what it means to claim that and to then argue about its validity with people who *do* experience racism in their daily lives*, and who don't have access to the kind of choices around it that you have. (I'm not saying you're white or that you should call yourself that. I'm only questioning use of the term *POC*.) Think about what it means to claim *a marginalized identity* when you don't have *a marginalized experience*. Really. Think about it. Don't just get offended and start crying about identity-policing. Really consider what that means.

Just a suggestion.

The bottom line here is that if you acknowledge your privilege and then just go ahead and do the same things anyhow, you have done absolutely zero things differently from people who don't acknowledge their privilege at all. Because the outcome is exactly the same. The impact is exactly the same.

It's also worth saying that I think we need to talk less about privilege altogether and more about supremacy. But that's another post.

In the meantime, when we do talk about privilege, I suggest we stop talking about "acknowledging" it and start focusing seriously on "pushing back against" it. Let's maybe make it a goal in 2014.

To the Queer Black Kids

Originally published May 2013

Y esterday I was stopped at a red light and I saw a little boy, maybe six years old, waiting with his mother to cross the street. The way he stood, with one hip jutted out and a hand on the other hip, filled me with happiness. He had very large eyes and long lashes and as he looked around, he seemed to take everything into his small self, his eyes bright with excitement over the woman selling strawberries on the corner, and the sounds coming from the barber shop. As they started to cross the street, as they started walking, the mother reached over and grabbed the boy's shoulder and said, "Stop walking *like that!*" The boy's entire demeanor changed. His shoulders rounded, his head lowered. I couldn't see his eyes anymore.

I thought about all the boxes black children are forced into. All children are forced into boxes, but for black children there is a particular urgency about it. When his mother said what she said, her voice sounded angry, cruel, but also scared. Because for black bodies, it's a matter of survival, always. I don't need to quote statistics. You know what I'm talking about. If you don't, then this message is not for you.

This message is for the queer black kids, queer in all kinds of ways, including but not limited to *different*, *gay*, *quirky*, *dykey*, and *fabulous*, who are learning right now that they shouldn't walk *like that*. Who are being told right now that there is shame in not being small enough to fit neatly into a box marked *boy* or *girl*. Who are being fooled into thinking that those boxes mean anything at all.

I want you to know I see you. With your hip out to one side. With your wide eyes. I want you to know that we are out here, too, that we were once you (in a way, because no one is exactly you), and we *know*.

We know how confusing it is when people talk about wanting you to be free, and then do everything they can to keep you from being free. We know what it is to wonder how freedom could possibly look like just the same old box.

Your mother may be trying to protect you. But hurting someone yourself to keep others from hurting them is really no kind of protection at all. I wish your mother knew that. I wish a lot of mother's knew it.

Anyway, I just want you to know that I am out here, that we are out here and that we love the way you walk. That it fills us with happiness to see you being who you are, whoever you are. That there are people who cross your path every day and come away better for it. That you are a gift.

Keep switchin' them hips.

How To Be A Reverse-Racist: A Step-By-Step List For Oppressing White People

Originally published June 2012

W hite people who are confronted with their white privilege and the white supremacist acts they perpetuate have been known to cry, "You're being a reverse-racist!" That is completely true: people of color have the power and control to create, perpetuate, and maintain brutal systematic reverse-racism that oppresses white people every day. As such, we have created this handy list on how to continue this oppression.

1. Enslave their bodies.

Ship them from Germany, Sweden, and other exotic countries. Force them to build entire cities, roads, bridges. Force them to plant and harvest all the food everyone eats. Let an entire economic system be built on their backs, with their blood and sweat. Later, deny them access to the system they have been used to build, and accuse them of being extremely lazy.

120

2. Steal their land.

If they were here before you, steal their land. This is essential. Basically, just go in there and take it. If you have to kill some of them to get it...no worries. If you have to kill almost all of them to get it...shit, no worries. After you steal their land, make sure you create laws to keep them from ever returning to it. If they try to return anyway, build fences, and let bands of POC vigilantes patrol the borders with guns. If they somehow get past the borders and into your country, no worries, you can always just deport them.

3. Enslave their minds.

From these systems, build a long lasting institution of reverse-racism until all the violence and microaggressions make many whites into depressed people with a lot of internalized self-hatred, health problems, and mental illnesses. Then deny them access to adequate mental health care. Or, adequate health care of any kind, while you're at it. 'Cause, you know, fuck 'em.

4. Wipe out and/or appropriate their customs.

Since many of their customs are savage and unworthy of pre-serving, wipe out their traditions of eating mashed potatoes and meatloaf, playing miniature golf, buying khakis at Banana Republic, and sleeping with thousand-count Egyptian cotton sheets. For the customs you think are kinda cool, culturally appropriate from them. Sometimes wear a beret and lederhosen, because Swedish culture is really exotic even though it's inferior to ours.

5. Break their espresso machines.

With baseball bats or large hammers. Or, you know, just unplug them all.

6. Call them "honky".

As people of color, we have been rightfully accused of being racist to white people, especially when we call them "honky". As we all know, calling them "honky" is egregiously offensive and horribly shocking because of this long, violent, reverse-racist history.

7. Just keep being terrible to them.

Do everything you can think of to make it so that white people make less money; their children are shot by cops; white women are at higher risk for assault and they are exotified until they no longer seem human; white men are beaten and thrown into jails because they look "suspicious" and "threatening"; they are racially profiled everywhere they go.

8. Make sure most representations of them in the media are negative.

They should almost always be portrayed as pasty, stringy-haired, rhythm-less, sexless, uptight, and booooring. Also, there should be very few representations of them and when they're portrayed at all, they should always only be the comic relief, the criminal, the silent exotic sex object, the Debbie Downer, or the incompetent sidekick. They are only allowed to be easily forgettable, one-dimensional characters. Sometimes use POC actors in white-face to portray these white people. By presenting this ONE image of them all the time, you will be able to convince the rest of the population that all white people are like this, thus ensuring a widespread belief in their inferiority.

9. Keep telling them how beautiful they are not.

White people know they will never be beautiful with their boring sour cream complexions and blonde hair (that was actually caused because of mutations). Plaster people of color on every magazine, show them in every television show and movie, and praise them as the most beautiful. When white people cry at these injustices, bottle their tears and sell them as health creams for people of color. Nothing like a soothing lotion made from the pain of white folks!

10. Go bananas!

Force them underground and away from the sun to become even whiter, while you laugh manically like the cruel, blood-thirsty, oppressive person of color you are! Take their thousand-count Egyptian cotton sheets to make POC-supremacist flags and hoods and march through the streets, spreading fear and terror. Every time a white person thinks your behavior is unfair or wrong, tell them that they should stop being so sensitive! We live in a post-reverse-racial society now! Jeez.

Afterthoughts:
This was one of *BGD*'s most popular early posts. It's gone viral several times. A little snark goes a long way. As long as it's built on legitimate points.

If I could wave a magic wand and eliminate one term from the lexicon of racism discussion, it would be "reverse-racism". It's the go-to of every clueless person who can't be bothered to take any time to understand anything about history or context. Every time I hear it, my faith in humanity diminishes. Use of that term is the easiest way to tell that someone has no idea what racism actually is. These are the same people who will, in response to a POC's complex and nuanced understanding of racism, quote the dictionary definition to us. They can't fathom that we know more about *our own experiences* than the *dictionary*.

'Reverse-racism' is not a thing. Tell your friends.

Calling In A Queer Debt

Originally published June 2013

Two days ago, the Supreme Court repealed the segment of the 1965 Voting Rights Act that functioned to guarantee that communities of color have equal access to voting rights as white communities. On the same day, the court dealt a blow to the 1978 Indian Child Welfare Act, a federal law intended to keep Native American children from being taken from their homes and typically adopted or fostered by non-Native American parents. Yesterday, that same Supreme Court struck down the Defense of Marriage Act and Proposition 8, clearing the way for LGBT couples to access marriage rights. It's possible that there has never been a week in the Supreme Court that so blatantly demonstrates which groups are a priority and which aren't when considering the lives and liberties of US citizens.

But that's not what this piece is about. There will (and should) be plenty of articles written today and in the coming days that highlight that reality. Check out the perspectives of the good folks at *Colorlines*, *Crunk Feminist Collective*, *Racialicious*, etc. now and in the coming days. I know I will be.

126

What this article is about is one thing: action.

This is a call to all the people who assured me and so many other people of color and queer people of color that even though they are happy about the repeal of DOMA, they are still very upset about the blow to the VRA. This is a call to all the race and/or class privileged folks who insist that it doesn't have to be an either/or, that they can rejoice in the new rights of LGBT people while at the same time raging over the further disenfranchisement of folks of color and poor folks, many of whom *are* LGBT. This is a call to all y'all.

This is a call for those of you who have said that gay is the new black. That gays not being able to get legally married was like black folks having to sit at the back of the bus. That the Marriage Rights Movement was the same as the Civil Rights Movement and why didn't black people see that?

This is a call to all of you who told undocumented queers and trans* activists not to talk about immigration status or wave trans pride flags because it wouldn't look good for your mainstream movement. This is a call to all of *you* who told all of *us* to wait. And wait. Until you got *yours*.

Well, now you have it.

It's Pride month. This coming weekend, San Francisco Pride will happen and other Prides will happen in New York, Seattle, Minneapolis, and in cities around the world. This is a great opportunity for all the people who have promised all these years that once gay marriage got its due they would then be able to focus on other issues that affect the more vulnerable citizens in our communities. This is your chance to MAKE GOOD.

Pride parades this weekend will be more heavily attended by the press than perhaps any in history. What will you do with the world watching? Will you cry tears of joy and laughter over the repeal of DOMA and never utter a word about the smashing of the Voting Rights Act? Or will you do what you have said you would do? Will you make room in your agenda for the rest of us? Those of us who are queer *and* black, trans* *and* Chicano, intersex *and* South Asian, and Two-Spirit? Will you speak up for us, while the cameras roll? Will you speak up for all the people in this country whose rights are being taken away while yours are being increased? Or will you be silent?

It is not enough to acknowledge your privilege. Acknowledging it will never make it better, will never, ever change anything. At some point, you must *act against it*. This is that point.

So, come on. Whatchu waiting for?

Am I A Bully? One Angry Black Woman's Reflection

Originally published September 2013

A few months ago, someone accused me of being a bully. Since it came from someone I don't trust, I dismissed it. Sometime later it came up again, in conversation with someone I do trust. At which point it became necessary to give it some serious thought.

I didn't, and don't, like the idea of being a bully. I, myself, was bullied as a kid. A skinny, awkward, bookish girl with a face that was mostly nose, I got teased a lot and sometimes pushed around, mostly by girls my own age who I'll refer to as "practice bullies," girls who weren't big-time thugs or anything, were often bullied themselves, and who saw my skinny, high-level-reading self as their chance to finally dominate someone. I put up with it. To a certain extent. Basically, I would let several snide comments, insults or threats go and hope they wouldn't continue. I was small and scared to fight and if I could avoid it, I would. But at the same time, I had my pride. I had my dignity. I was scared of fighting, but more scared still of being pushed around endlessly, of being victimized.

Sticking up for yourself is incredibly important in black culture and black life. It is deeply ingrained in our legacies of resistance to oppression. You cannot stick up for yourself as a slave, so for centuries upon centuries, black people in this country had almost no recourse against the neverending onslaught of violence and degradation perpetrated against us. When my people could not fight back in many of the ways they may have wanted to, they found other ways. This included everything from "losing" a necessary tool needed to get some plantation task completed on a certain day to slowly poisoning the master's food to running away. It was all they had. After slavery ended, and Jim Crow kicked in, our options opened up a tiny bit. But there has never been a time in the history of black people in this country when sticking up for ourselves didn't hold with it the possibility of our death, even today (see: Trayvon Martin). It doesn't stop us from doing it, though. It is part of who we are. And I knew that, even as kid.

So, when someone bullied me, I'd draw a line in the sand. I'd say to myself, "Okay, Mia, the next time [insert girl's name here] says some shit/gets in my face, I'm going to call her out." In my day, in my neighborhood, "calling out" meant challenging someone to a fight. And that's what I would do. The next time Lisa or Halimah or Yasmin or whoever started talking shit to me, I'd put my foot down. I'd call her out. Not because I wanted to fight, but because I felt I had to. There is a famous story among my childhood friends detailing an incident when I arrived at the door of my eighth-grade frienemy (who had called me a dyke at school and was talking mad shit behind my back) and politely asked her mother if she was at home, and then when said frienemy appeared at the door, I said, chest all puffed out, "I'm sick of your shit. You got all that talk, now back it up. Come out and fight me." She wouldn't come out, no matter how many times I insisted. Talk, as it turns out, was all she had. I eventually went back home, feeling vindicated. She never called me names or talked shit about me again. That's usually how those situations went. I always felt proud of myself for refusing to be pushed around, for sticking up for myself even though I was afraid. I was proud to be that kind of nerd.

The few times that kind of thing happened over my childhood years were probably the only times when anyone perceived me as intimidating. In the context of West Philadelphia kid life, I was never that. Among inner-city black kids, I present as the bookish nerd that I am. It wasn't until I left that environment, and especially until I was around a lot of white people, that the idea of me being "intimidating" started to come up. I got whiffs of it here and there, from one white girl or another, but it was so far outside any scope of identity I held for myself and so far outside my own people's experience of me that it was almost impossible for me to believe it and it took me years and years to even accept that it was true and *why* it was true (hint: anti-black racism + misogyny = misogynoir). In those years, many white women told me I looked "mean." That I wasn't "friendly." I was accused of "bitchiness." And so on. Whenever I asserted myself in any way, even when I was intentionally being super-nice about it, I was intimidating. If I wasn't completely in agreement with someone's opinion or just shutting up altogether, I was "argumentative." I saw white women, and even light-skinned women of color, behaving the same way, and even more assertively than I was, and nobody was "intimidated" by it. And, Lord, don't let me *actually* get angry. Don't let me raise my voice even a quarter of an octave, because then I was some kind of raging black bitch monster scaring the shit out of all the civilized people who know how to communicate non-violently. Jesus. I mean, really. My choices were to be silent and pushed around, or speak up for myself and be perceived as too aggressive, mean or violent. It's the story of a black girl's life. It is tiresome. And it is the reason I started BGD in the first place.

But still. The reason I got to thinking about this "bully" thing in the first place was that a friend of mine who I love kinda sorta gently suggested that I might have tendencies which could be experienced as bullying by *some* people. Honestly, it freaked me out when she said it, because that's not who I see myself as or want to be. But I am deeply committed to self-reflection, so as freaked out as I was, I seriously considered it. I went onto the internets and the googles and the whatnots and did a search: Am I A Bully? I read hella stuff about it and what I came to is this: a bully is someone who dominates people for the sake of domination. Basically, bullies get off on making people feel dominated. I can say with 100% certainty that does not describe me.

But. Here's where it gets tricky.

Recently, I had a conversation with a couple of friends wherein they explained to me that I have power. Apparently, as a somewhat well-known QPOC, I have *influence* and shit like that. It took a while for them to convince me of this. Even with BGD's popularity, even with all of the amazing things I've been able to do in the past year and a half, I still see myself as that awkward kid who doesn't belong. So, while I might understand intellectually that I have some power and influence in my particular community, it doesn't necessarily feel that way in my little nerd soul. In my little nerd soul, I am still that kid. Even when I am raging against oppression at the top of my lungs, even when I am checking assholes who presume to tell me about my own experience as a black woman, even when I am saying a heartfelt fuck you to a whole lot of people on these internets, I am still that kid. Doing what I must do to demand respect when people try to deny me respect. Standing up for myself and my people. Never, at least in my own perception, am I wielding power. That's not what the psyche of a nerdy black girl looks like. Not any nerdy black girl I know, anyway.

Still, whether it's because they legitimately see me as having power, or because they illegitimately perceive me as being more aggressive and mean by default because I'm a black woman, or both, *other people*–nine times of out ten white and other non-black people–sometimes see me differently.

The question for me is, how much of this is my problem and how much is other people's racist and misogynist shit? The answer is: some and a lot.

My problem:

A while back, I wrote a short piece called "On Getting Free," in which I say that there are tools for survival that each of us has and that these tools helped us...well, survive. But that at some point, after we grew up and built relatively "safe" lives for ourselves, we stopped needing these particular tools. Only we never stopped using them. And while they helped us survive, they actually get in the way of us getting free, which is a very different thing. I think for me, this way that I have of asserting my little nerd self, of puffing up my chest and putting down my foot in order to protect myself and not be victimized, is one such tool. And for me, it's not so much that I don't need it anymore, because a black woman always needs a tool like that, rather it's that there are places in my life where I need it and places where I don't. There are places where it serves me and places where it doesn't. And I need to really understand and keep in mind which places are which. Battling a queerphobic, racist, classist, misogynist world: right place. Interpersonal relationships: not so much. And when dealing with people (friends, family, lovers, people I want to build community with) whose past personal traumas make them easily triggered by assertive personalities (as in the case of the dear friend whose suggestion started me on this "bully" quest), I need to find gentler ways to approach conflict with them. (And they, as adults, traumatized or not, are also responsible for the ways in which they do or do not engage in healthy communication with me).

Also: the truth is that, whether I'm comfortable with it or not, I *do* have power. And it's my responsibility to be careful and cognizant about how I use it.

Other people's racist/misogynistic shit:

Is their problem.

A few weeks ago, a friend reminded me that many, many black women bloggers have stopped writing because the sheer volume of racism and misogyny directed at them was just too much for any person to handle. I don't think anyone who is not a black woman can even *begin* to imagine how much hatred is directed towards us when we dare to say *anything* in public, let alone when we are demanding respect. There are many, many people in the world who don't even see us as *human*. Do y'all get that?

I started BGD because I got sick and tired of being told that as a black woman I could never assert myself without being perceived as aggressive. That I could never stand up for myself without being perceived as mean. That I could never draw a line past which I would not allow myself to be mistreated without being perceived as violent. It's a decision I do not regret. And when anyone dismisses all of that in favor of an easy "bully" label, they are undermining the power and righteousness of those intentions. It's like when women of any color stand up and fight and demand respect and are dismissed by men as having "penis-envy." It is people projecting racist and misogynist ideas onto someone in order to take the light off themselves and their own inability to be accountable for the harm that they cause. It's a disgustingly easy out.

I have been able to do everything that I have been able to do precisely because I refuse to become smaller in order to accommodate other people's anti-black racism and misogyny. That's not me being a bully. That's me refusing to *be bullied*.

I am not a bully. I am an assertive black woman who is kind and caring and generous, but who's not taking *anybody's* shit. There is a difference.

So, instead of easy-outs, how about hearing black women out? How about making space for black women, how about giving us a break every now and again? How about responding with compassion when you see black women trying to defend ourselves, however clumsily, against *constant* attacks, the horribleness of which you can't even begin to know? How about **hearing our hurt** and responding with love and care and accountability?

How about that?

No More 'Allies'

Originally published September 2013

I'm kinda over the term "ally." Between Tim Wise's recent (but not new) bullshit, a recent visit to a college where some so-called allies don't even understand basic racism 101, and the constant cookie-seeking of people who just can't do the right thing unless they are sure they're gonna get some kind of credit for it, I'm done.

Allyship is not supposed to look like this, folks. It's not supposed to be about you. It's not supposed to be about your feelings. It's not supposed to be a way of glorifying yourself at the expense of the folks you claim to be an ally to. It's not supposed to be a performance. It's supposed to be a way of living your life that doesn't reinforce the same oppressive behaviors you're claiming to be against. It's supposed to be about you doing the following things:

1. shutting up and listening
2. educating yourself (you could start with the thousands of books and websites that already exist and are chock

full of damn near everything anyone needs to know about most systems and practices of oppression)

3. when it's time to talk, not talking over the people you claim to be in solidarity with

4. accepting feedback/criticism about how your "ally-ship" is causing more harm than good without whitesplaining/mansplaining/whateversplaining

5. shutting up and listening some more

6. supporting groups, projects, orgs, etc. run by and for marginalized people so our voices get to be the loudest on the issues that effect us

7. not expecting marginalized people to provide emotional labor for you

This is by no means a comprehensive list. But most "allies" aren't even getting these things right.

So, henceforth, I will no longer use the term "ally" to describe anyone. Instead, I'll use the phrase "currently operating in solidarity with." Or something. I mean, yeah, it's clunky as hell. But it gets at something that the label of "ally" just doesn't. And that's this: actions count; labels don't.

"Currently operating in solidarity with" is undeniably an action. It describes what a person is doing in the moment. It does not give credit for past acts of solidarity without regard for current behavior. It does not assume future acts of solidarity. It speaks only to the actions of the present. Some other options:

- showing support for…
- operating with intentionality around…
- using my privilege to help by…
- demonstrating my commitment to ending [insert oppressive system] by…
- showing up for [insert marginalized group] in the following ways…

These are all better ways of talking about–and thinking about–allyship because they are active, and because they require examples. This is key. Why? Because, as I and countless others have said many, many times, allyship is an every day practice. The work of an ally is never ceasing. As long as the isms are functioning–and they are functioning at full capacity every hour of every day–then the action of allyship must function just as perpetually, just as fully, just as tirelessly.

"Ally" cannot be a label that someone stamps onto you–or, god forbid, that you stamp on to yourself—so you can then go around claiming it as some kind of identity. It's not an identity. It's a practice. It's an active thing that must be done over and over again, in the largest and smallest ways, every day.

Sounds like a lot of work, huh? Sounds exhausting. Well, yeah, it ought to. Because the people who experience racism, misogyny, ableism, queerphobia, transphobia, classism, etc. are exhausted. So, why shouldn't their "allies" be?

Maybe how exhausted you are is a good measure of how well you're doing the work.

On Defending Beyoncé: Black Feminists, White Feminists, and the Line In the Sand

Originally published December 2013

Last Friday, Beyoncé dropped a new, super-secret self-titled album and my Facebook feed promptly lost its mind. There were so many people talking about it that I had to see what was up. I watched all of the videos. And while I can't say that most of the songs are thrilling, many of the videos are pretty fantastic. I was pretty entertained all around. Satisfied, I went ahead and moved on.

But then. The black feminist blogosphere started showing up hard for Bey, defending her to all the white feminists who have thrown shade over the years and everybody from Mikki Kendall to *Crunk Feminist Collective* was declaring Bey a feminist. Like for sure. Like, seriously, why are y'all still questioning this?

In her piece for the Guardian, entitled, "Beyoncé's New Album Should Silence Her Feminist Critics," Mikki wrote, "This album makes it clear that her feminism isn't academic; isn't about waves, or labels. It simply is a part of her as much as anything else in her life. She's pro-woman without being anti-man, and she wants the world to know that you can be feminist on a personal level without sacrificing emotions, friendships or fun."

Okay. I respect Mikki Kendall. She's super smart and usually hella on point. I'm not really sure why she's only talking about Beyonce's "personal" feminism. (In fact, she goes on to say a lot about the pop star's personal life and what's feminist about it without ever saying much about her public persona and what she's putting out there with that. Which is weird.) But, yeah, there are obvious feminist themes in the song/video for "Pretty Hurts". And "***Flawless" has some feminist themes as well. And there is almost nothing happening here that is anti-feminist. (Almost. We'll get back to that in just a bit.)

So, while I'm not sure that one or two feminist songs on an album with 14 tracks is really a feminist triumph that should silence all critics (also, the pessimist in me is like: this is corporate entertainment, "feminism" added to get people talking and thus sell more records), I do see Beyoncé as a kind of feminist. Not just because of this album, but because of feminist things she has said in the past that reveal her analysis. She's not a perfect feminist (none of us are), she still has a way to go (most of us do), but she is a feminist.

However. There are some legit concerns. Here's my biggest issue with the album:

In her new song "Drunk In Love, " featuring her husband, Jay-Z, he raps the following lines:

"Catch a charge, I might, beat the box up like Mike" and "Baby know I don't play...I'm Ike Turner...now eat the cake Anna Mae."

In case you're not up on your wife-beater trivia, that second line is a reference to an infamous incident in the verbally, physically, psychologically and sexually abusive marriage of Ike and Tina Turner wherein Ike forced Tina (Anna Mae) to eat cake by smashing it in her face.

Um, what?

It was one of the last videos I watched and after some legit pro-woman awesomeness, it felt like a slap in the face. A very intentional one. In the middle of this big ol' so-called feminist triumph, Jay-Z pops in to glorify violence against women and...that's just cool with Bey, New Black Feminist Superhero of the Universe? And everybody else, too?

I guess so, because over on Crunk Feminist Collective's blog, Crunktastic is writing stuff like:

"I'm here for anybody that is checking for the f-word, since so many folk aren't. (Except Republicans. Ain't nobody here for that.) What we look like embracing Queen Latifah and Erykah Badu even though they patently reject the term, but shading and policing Bey who embraces it? If Bey is embracing this term, that is laudable."

No shade to the homies at CFC. But are we really arguing that calling yourself a feminist while allowing your husband to spit incredibly disgusting anti-woman shit alongside you on your album is just as legit as not calling yourself a feminist while demonstrating consistent feminist ideals? Because I have to respectfully disagree. I rarely embrace the term feminist. It often feels too disconnected from my particular experience as a black woman. But while I often reject the term itself, my ideals, my politics, and the work I put out into the world does reflect those values. The idea that embracing the term is all by itself laudable is a serious stretch.

Another stretch: there has also been much made of the fact that Beyoncé samples Chimamanda Ngozi Adichie on her track "***Flawless." She tells bitches to "bow down" to her over a recording of Adichie talking about feminism.

Adichie quotes a dictionary definition of a feminist as "a person who believes in the social, economic and political equality of the sexes." This seems to be Beyoncé's way of declaring herself a feminist. I like the quote, I think it's important, and I'm really glad it's there. That said: I think it sets the bar just a bit too low. I would argue that, with all due respect to the dictionary, that definition is lacking in one very important sense. I would add:

...and who is able to look at the world with a critical eye so as to be able to identify those times and places where that equality is not present.

Believing in the equality of the sexes while having no consistent analysis that makes you able to identify when and where inequality is actually taking place (for example: in a line about Ike Turner humiliating and abusing his wife) is not being a feminist. Because I don't believe that feminism is just about what you think society should ideally be like, but rather how you both perceive society as it is and how you push back against its real injustices. In fact, Ms. Adichie herself defines feminism as "A man or a woman who says, 'Yes, there is a problem with gender as it exists today and we must fix it; we must do better.'" It's great that Bey gets that women getting paid less is some bullshit. But it's also really important to not let your husband rap about abusing women on your "feminist" album.

Kendall writes: "Feminism has never been one size fits all, yet much of the criticism that revolves around entertainers like Beyoncé...presumes that there is a unilateral guide on how to be the "right" kind of feminist."

Sure, there isn't one way to be a feminist. There aren't two ways or ten ways. But the fact that there are many ways to be a feminist does not and should not suggest that all ways are feminist ways. Feminism may be many things, but it isn't all things. You can't do and say things that are anti-woman (or allow your husband to do so alongside you on your album) and claim feminism at the same time. I mean, if we can agree on just one thing about feminism, it should be that you can't glorify the marital abuses of Ike Turner and be a feminist.

I'm here for black feminists defending Beyoncé against criticisms that she does not deserve. But I also hope that we can call out the flaws in her feminist expressions. I understand that at some point, the Beyoncé feminist/non-feminist discussion became a line in the sand, a line past which we were no longer prepared to let white feminists go. Black feminists, black women, have had to deal with constant disrespect from white feminists, not just over Beyoncé but over so, so many black women and girls and at this point we are just really fucking tired of it. We defend Beyoncé because she is a symbol of the ways in which white feminists degrade, dehumanize and demonize black women all the damn time. She is an easy example of the ways white feminists ignore and exclude black women from "their" movements, the way they paint our experiences as secondary and inferior to their own, the way they other our sexuality and demean our right to own it. We defend her against white feminists because we know that we are the only ones who can and the only ones who will. We defend her because, feminist or not, she is our sister, our daughter, our girlfriend. We defend her because having the back of a black

147

woman being attacked by white folks is, in and of itself, part of our feminism.

We fully understand that much of what white feminists have said about Beyoncé has been in line with the same misogynoirist language and attitudes that white feminists have been displaying towards black women since...well, forever. We hear the code words, we see the upturned noses. Our ways of being in the world have never been good enough for white feminists. We defend Beyoncé because she is one of us, she is of us, and we're not about to turn our backs while white women do to her what they have done to us throughout history.

Okay. I'm here for that. I'm here for defending Beyoncé's right to own her sexuality and make no apologies for it. I'm here for defending her right to figure out who she is and what she believes without having to answer to every white feminist who thinks she's not figuring it out fast enough. I'm here for all of that. What I'm not here for is pretending that Beyoncé is some champion of black feminism as some kind of "up yours" to white women, especially if it means ignoring seriously problematic things. Frankly, I think we can do a whole lot better than that. I think—I hope—we can defend Beyoncé in all the legitimate ways there are to do so (and there are many) without losing our sense of what black feminism really is, in all of its complexities, and what it's really not (see again: Ike Turner). I hope—I really hope—we can love Beyoncé and stand up for her without giving her, or ourselves, or anyone else, a pass.

One of my favorite scenes in all of Beyonce's new videos is in "Partition" when she drops that napkin just so that white woman has to pick it up. I read it as an incredible moment wherein a powerful black woman flips the script on white women who are constantly trying to put her in "her place" and in one subtle movement puts them in theirs. And I am all for black women pushing back against white feminist nonsense. But it should not happen at the expense of a black feminism that includes keeping our critical lens focused, not just on white women and others who would seek to tear us down, but also on our idols and ourselves.

On Colbert and White Racial Satire: We Don't Need It

Originally published April 2014

A lot of strange things have happened since *The Colbert Report* tweeted a line from a skit that Stephen Colbert did on his show last week about Dan Snyder's new 'R—skins' Foundation, wherein he attempted to highlight the absurdity and offensiveness of it by invoking racial slurs against Asians. Many Asian American activists, led by freelance writer Suey Park, have pushed back against Colbert and the offending joke by calling for the show's cancellation with a Twitter hashtag—#CancelColbert—that went viral last Thursday night. In response, Colbert fans have defended him, some of them respectfully and many of them—in particular white men on Twitter—with racist slurs and rape and death threats directed towards the activists, most of them young Asian women, who called Colbert out.

The horrifying behavior of so many of the white men defending Colbert is not the focus of this piece, but I do want to say this: it's disgusting and dangerous and downright criminal and it needs to stop. If we've learned anything in the age of social media, it's that people will say anything when they can do it anonymously and not have to look you in the eye. Making threats from behind a keyboard takes zero courage, which is why it's the preferred pastime of so many assholes. But let's not let that reality cause us to not take these threats seriously. They are serious and the people making them should be held accountable.

What I'm interested in here, though, is the response of people of color to this Colbert debacle.

Let me say here that I wouldn't have called myself a huge fan of *The Colbert Report*. But I've watched it plenty over the years and often found it amusing. I think Colbert is good, and often great, at poking fun at the conservative blowhards he's satirizing. I think he sometimes goes too far, particularly when using racial satire, and it's those jokes in particular that I'm critiquing here, or rather people's defense of them.

I've seen a lot of POC, Asian American and otherwise, come out hard in Colbert's defense, often while throwing the Asian American activists and others who called him out under the bus. (Yes, we *do* understand it was satire. Yes, we *can* take a joke. And yes, we are *still* offended. All of those things can happen at the same time.) I don't really understand why so many of us are defending him. Not because people of color are a monolith who are all supposed to think the same things and react the same ways, but because I just don't get why we're so invested in white racial satire.

What do I mean when I say invested? I mean that you believe that *The Colbert Report* and white racial satire (on *SNL*, *Chelsea Lately*, etc.) are important and/or necessary and that you are willing to defend them.

Whether you like *The Colbert Report* or not, whether you were offended by that joke or not, the question I'm asking is why anyone—particularly people of color—is *invested* in *The Colbert Report* in particular and in white racial satire in general. What is white racial satire *doing* for us that is so important? Important enough to outright dismiss, at best, and rail against, at worse, people who speak out when they are harmed by it?

If your answer is "free speech" please have a seat and think harder. Free speech is rarely the reason anyone defends anything with this kind of vigor. Free speech is the go-to when you're already behind something someone said and you need an argument for why. My question is why are you behind it to begin with? You can be for free speech and not be invested in white racial satire. Believing that Colbert has a right to say what he wants does not require you to get up in arms when someone is offended by it.

I haven't gotten any solid answers from POC who defend Colbert about why they are so invested. They either say that they aren't (while continuing to defend the show) or they say something along the lines of, "he helps POC sometimes." How he helps POC...well, no one seems to be quite sure. He's definitely not helping us by hiring us.

Some people have suggested that *The Colbert Report* is fighting racism...somehow. That by taking on the persona of a conservative a-hole, Colbert is calling attention to how ridiculous they are. Yes. Ok. But calling attention to whom, and for what purpose? The fans who have responded angrily to #CancelColbert have either been liberals who believe they are in on the joke already or tweeting lunatics who seem to just get pleasure from hearing and hurling racial slurs. Where are these theoretical people who were racist until they watched *Colbert*, or *SNL*, or *Chelsea Lately*, or any other show that uses white racial satire, and had their racist minds changed? Do we really believe these people exist? Do we really believe there were hella people watching Colbert's skit about Dan Snyder's awful foundation who had their minds changed about it as soon as Asian slurs were thrown into the mix? Do we really think folks who defend that team's name despite of all the harm it's caused to Native people are sensitive to the stereotyping of Asian people? You're telling me these folks exist?

And, you know what, even if they did, why is their "education-in-the-form-of-racist-jokes-that-are-satirical-so-it's-okay" more important than the people we know for sure exist who are harmed by these jokes?

I reject the idea that we "need" white racial satire. That it's helping us somehow. That it's so powerful a tool against oppression that without it we can never end racism. That POC should be grateful for it, because these white people making "ching chong" jokes, in the case of Colbert, and jokes about black men's penises, in the case of Chelsea Handler, are on our side and somehow making our lives better with their humor. That's some especially convoluted white savior nonsense. And really, if the white savior narrative had any validity at all (which it doesn't), it wouldn't have it in the form of Chelsea Handler, ok?

Consider for a moment, folks, that *The Colbert Report* isn't the best we can hope for. That it isn't the best we can do. That we don't need it. And that it's white supremacy (with a heaping helping of patriarchy and male privilege) that tries to convince us otherwise, that tells us that anything white people do to us is okay, as long as they say they're helping.

If folks put a fifth of the energy they are spending defending Colbert into calling and emailing Dan Snyder and company to demand they change the name of the Washington team in support of Native people, that would be the subject of a dozen ma-

154

jor news outlet's stories instead of this. If people put that same energy into supporting POC comedians like W. Kamau Bell, Hari Kondabolu, Gloria Bigelow, Pia Glenn, and so many others to control our own narratives, TV would already look a lot different than it does.

We don't need white racial satire. Let's invest in something else.

Six Things You're Probably Doing To Further Inequality

New 2014

L et's just jump right into it, shall we?

1. Not educating yourself about the realities of oppression

We live under a system of white supremacist capitalist patriar-chy. That system isn't set up to educate you about the realities of oppression. Quite the contrary. White supremacist capitalist patriarchy wants you to believe it's not even there, that it's not even operating. The only way to understand the nuances of oppression is to take the time to educate yourself.

Most people don't bother to educate themselves. If you ask them, these people will often tell you that they care about "equality" or some other general idea. But they've never taken any steps to educate themselves about the myriad ways ine-quality actually functions. This, of course, doesn't stop them from arguing with marginalized people about oppression. I mean, why should total ignorance of a subject prevent you from dominating a conversation about it, right? (Wrong.)

Educating yourself and other privileged people is important work. It takes the burden of your education off of marginalized people, where it never belonged in the first place. If you're not educating yourself and others like you, you're not really helping.

2. Second-guessing marginalized people about their experiences of marginalization

I gave a keynote in Toronto last winter at an event called *Queering Black History Month*. During a panel discussion, for which I was an audience member, one of the panelists, a queer, masculine of center person, said that they identify as a cyborg because, as a black person in Canada, that's how they feel. During the Q&A, a white man stood up and said that he didn't think they should identify that way because blackness can exist without separating itself from humanity. The panelist, rightly, told him to go fuck himself, in so many words.

I cannot even begin to imagine the sense of entitlement it takes for a white guy to stand up in a room full of black folks at a black event and tell a black person how they should identify in connection with their blackness! Unfortunately, though, this happens all the time. Privileged people are constantly questioning, second-guessing, and offering their opinions to marginalized people about our identities and experiences. We say something racist happened, they say, "No...I don't think that's what it was."

It should go without saying that oppressed people know the most about experiences of oppression. The idea that people who never experience an "ism" know more about it than people who experience it every day is preposterous. If you don't experience a particular form of oppression, don't second-guess people who do.

3. Talking about "diversity" without talking about oppression

This phenomenon is especially epidemic in schools, particularly colleges and universities. The word "diversity" is thrown around: used in brochures and on college websites with glossy pictures of black and brown students smiling in lab goggles or holding tennis rackets or whatever. Schools recruit black and brown students in the name of diversity and within a few months those students are buckling under the weight of white supremacy in classrooms, in clubs, and in every facet of their college experience. That's around the time they discover that there is no system in place to talk about *oppression*. To talk about racism or classism, especially.

The truth is that efforts toward diversity by itself do not produce a healthy or safe environment for students of color (or any other POC). Oppression and diversity can and do exist simultaneously. If you want to support the students of color whose success it is your job to support, then you need to make space to talk openly and honestly about, and take action against, oppression and, in particular, white supremacy, within your institutions.

Diversity is easy. You just throw a few different kinds of people together in one place and *voila!*—you've got diversity. Addressing oppression is much harder, heavier, uglier. And it is absolutely necessary.

4. White-washing history

White-washing history is the practice of de-radicalizing, by revision or omission, a historical figure or movement. It's basically taking the radical words, ideas and actions of historical anti-oppression movements, siphoning out the anger, the rage, the truth, and replacing it with something easier, something more palatable for privileged ears and consciences to accept. One of the most white-washed figures in the history of civil rights is Martin Luther King. Today, King is often painted as little more than a wise preacher who dreamed of a day when black folks and white folks could hold hands and sing spirituals together. In fact, King was a radical. He was thought of that way in his day, which is why he was hated and ultimately as-sassinated. According to Coretta Scott King, her husband went to jail *twenty-nine times*. All the while talking about the triple evils of poverty, racism and war. And yet the same institutions, politicians and corporations who uphold racism, poverty and war invoke his name and his dreams for their agendas.

The problem with white-washing isn't just that it misrepresents radical visionaries like King, which is bad enough, but that in doing so, it promotes a preferred approach to anti-oppression that is concerned with the comfort of the oppressor and not the lived realities of the oppressed. It pretends that the greatest struggles against oppression were "progressive" or "liberal," that our people asked nicely and that the oppressor, out of the goodness of his heart, heard us and made changes. This is a dangerously false revision of history that serves to sedate our movements. In truth, all of what has been gained through anti-oppression movements has been gained with voices as angry as they were calm, as full of rage as they were full of love. Rage has always been part of the fight against the dehumanizing forces of oppression. To deny that, and to cher-ry-pick the words of our leaders and the actions of our coura-geous people, who fought and died in those struggles, is appal-ling and anyone who does it—any politician, any corporation, any university, should be ashamed.

5. Navel-gazing about your privilege

Acknowledging your privilege is all the rage these days. The fact is, though, when you acknowledge your privilege you've done exactly zero things to combat oppression. Your acknowledgement of inequality doesn't do anything to level the playing field, which is the only way to move towards equality. Navel-gazing about your privilege is just another way to centralize your privileged self while simultaneously taking no action in the fight against oppression, thus ensuring that oppression continues as usual. It is not enough to acknowledge your privilege. You must actively push back against it. (See "4 Ways To Push Back Against Your Privilege" for a few examples.)

6. Tone-Policing

Tone-policing comes from the idea that oppressed people are only allowed to talk about oppression in a tone that is acceptable to privileged people. You enter any discussion on racism, sexism, ableism, transphobia, etc. and you will find people insisting that if we only said it nicer, they'd listen. In fact, it's our fault they don't listen, because we're too angry. If we really cared about getting our message across, we'd calm down and speak softer and be nicer. This thinking is problematic and dangerous for so many reasons.

First, it once again puts the focus, not on the very real *experiences* of oppressed people, but on the *feelings* of privileged people. How someone feels when being confronted about their racist words or actions is more important than the experience of racism the confronter has had to endure. So, not only are we expected to deal with whatever racist thing someone said or did, not only do we have to carry the often enormous weight of that, we also have to be sure to be careful about how we talk to them about it. Because…their feelings.

Second, it's a lie. The truth is that we have said it every way it can possibly be said already. We've said it the Ghandi way, we've said it the Malcolm X way, and we've said it every way in between. If saying it nicely was the key, we'd all be free by now. Each and every black person who goes out of their way to not make white people feel bad about their racism would be basking in the warmth of a post-racial society, rather than having their sons and brothers and sisters shot down by cops and vigilantes like dogs in the street. Maybe Trayvon Martin, Rekia Boyd, Oscar Grant and so many others would still be alive if we just said it nicer. Right?

It's a lie. A gross, insidious, dangerous lie.

Don't police the tone of other oppressed people and don't police your own. It is for each individual person, trying to survive under the enormous weight of oppression, to talk about it in whatever way they see fit. It is privilege and supremacy that makes people believe otherwise.

People who care about freedom, really care about it, more than their own comfort, more than their own ego, people who are ready to hear you, will hear you, even in your rage. Especially then.

This has not been a comprehensive list. There are probably many other things you're doing to further inequality. You can use this as a place to start. The more you do the work of educating yourself on these and other tools of oppression, the more you'll be able to identify ways to do better.

How To Be Black In America:
A (Relatively) Short List

Originally published August 2013

1 . Don't sag your pants. Pull them up. *Slowly*. Don't make any sudden movements.

2. Stop talking about racism. That's over. (see: black President)

2.5. Stop asking the black President to do anything to help you. That's reverse-racism. Or something.

3. Don't be mad.

4. Don't reach for your wallet. Or your cell phone.

5. *Who told you it was okay to walk down the street??*

6. Don't assert yourself. You're scaring people. Don't scare people so much.

7. Why do you talk like that?

8. Get an education somehow. Speak properly, for Christ's sake. But don't be uppity.

9. Why do you talk like *that*?

10. Don't wear a weave.

10.5. Don't wear your hair natural, either, unless you got that good hair. JP Morgan Chase don't do nappy.

11. Don't exist.

12. You're really dark. Can you do something about that? In fact, if you're going to insist on being black, please be as light-skinned as possible. Have a white parent, if you can manage it. K?

13. Jump.

14. Don't have kids unless you're married. And everyone knows Black women can't find husbands so... just don't have kids. If you must have them, though, have daughters.

14.5 Don't have sons. If you do have sons and they end up dead or in a cage, that's your problem. You should have known better.

15. Vote Democrat.

16. Don't talk about liking fried chicken. We are respectable negroes up in here.

17. Separate yourself as much as possible from niggers. Denounce *those* black people as often as you can.

18. Be nicer. You know people are intimidated by you, right? Why are you making it harder on yourself?

19. Be successful somehow. But do it without any kind of help. I mean, that's how white people did it, right? No help whatsoever.

20. Jesus, slavery was 150 years ago. Get your shit together.

21. Don't get nominated for an Oscar at 9 years old. This makes you a cunt.

22. Why is your name so weird? Imma just call you... (see: #21)

23. Let people who don't experience anti-black racism tell you what it is and what it is not, how it does and does not effect you, and how you should feel and, especially, *not feel* about it.

24. Tell people what aisle they can find the Ajax in. Because you obviously stock shelves at this Target even though you are wearing a suit.

25. *Why is your butt like that?*

26. If you're black and queer, choose which of those communities to align yourself with. I think the choice is obvious. (see: Recent Supreme Court Rulings)

27. Don't run. Unless you're on a football field. Black people running = something bad is happening. Unless it's sports.

28. Can your dick be smaller? I mean, you're kind of feeding into the stereotype with that thing.

29. Spend 98% of your energy trying to be more respectable/acceptable. Translation: why aren't you better at being a civilized human being?

30. Play dead. Learn to curl up in a ball as if trying to survive a bear attack.

31. Just get over it. White people with neck tattoos get discriminated against, too. It's not just you.

32. Don't defend yourself. Other people get to decide how you die. Accept that.

33. Remember that none of these things will necessarily save you. If you let yourself believe they will, that's your fault.

34. Hold close to your family and your homies, anyway. Make food with them. Cry. Laugh. Dance. Repeat. It may not save you, but it'll feel good.

34.5. Make crazy good, life-altering art.

35. Forgive somebody who looks like you.

36. Read a lot of books. Get recommendations from the baddest literary badasses you know.

37. Try really hard to get on a jury.

38. Reject ableism and cissexism and heteronormativity and classism and fat-shaming and normative gender roles and misogynoir and everything massa ever told you and is still telling you.

39. Keep going. Or don't.

39.5. Keep fighting. Or don't.

40. Look hard at your own individual shit and fix it so you can be better at love.

41. Love.

42. Don't forget about love.

ACKNOWLEDGEMENTS

I'd love to acknowledge everyone who has influenced me as a writer and a conscious queer black woman, but that's impossible. The best I can do is name the few who represent the many: Mary McKenzie, my mother and the first writer in my life; Doris, Charles, Sarah and Frances Wright, and Sarah Scott, my grandparents, aunts, and great-grandmother, respectively, whose love and pride made me who I am; Janie Lucas, my second- and third-grade teacher, who made me understand I was exceptional; Marilyn Boston, my sixth-grade teacher, who helped solidify my love of writing; all of the teachers whose classrooms were spaces of radical discourse; and all of the radical thinkers, especially the black women writers, whose brilliance continues to light my way.

Thank you.

RECOMMENDATIONS

Want more smart, bold commentary about race and/or queerness and/or class and/or gender? I highly recommend:

CarmenLeah Ascencio

Sydette Harry—Black Amazon

Jamie Nesbitt Golden—Hood Feminism

Jay Smooth—Ill Doctrine

Lauren Chief Elk—Save Wiyabi Project

Trudy—Gradient Lair

Suey Park

Shaadi Edwards (@tgirlinterruptd)

Robert Jones—Son of Baldwin

Edward Ndopu

Lisa J. Ellwood—The "Right" Kind of Brown

Daniel José Older

ABOUT THE AUTHOR

Mia McKenzie is a writer and a smart, scrappy Philadelphian (now living in Oakland) with a deep love of vegan pomegranate ice cream and fake fur collars. She studied writing at the University of Pittsburgh. She's the winner of the 2009 Astraea Foundation Writers Fund Award and the 2011 Leeway Foundation Transformation Award. Her debut novel, *The Summer We Got Free*, won the 2013 Lambda Literary Award. It was described by *Lambda Literary Review* as, "achingly poignant, laser-like in its facility and effect." You can read her short stories in *The Kenyon Review* and *make/shift*. She speaks about race, queerness, class, gender and the intersections of all of these at universities and conferences across the country. Read more about Mia at www.miamckenzie.net